C Internals
For
Coding Interviews

By
Kamal Rawat
Meenakshi

FIRST EDITION 2019

Copyright © BPB Publications, INDIA

ISBN : 978-93-8817-654-5

Distributors:

BPB PUBLICATIONS
20, Ansari Road, Darya Ganj
New Delhi-110002
Ph: 23254990/23254991

BPB BOOK CENTRE
376 Old Lajpat RaiMarket,
Delhi-110006
Ph: 23861747

MICRO MEDIA
Shop No. 5, Mahendra Chambers, 150
DN Rd. Next to Capital Cinema, V.T.
(C.S.T.) Station, MUMBAI-400 001
Ph: 22078296/22078297

DECCAN AGENCIES
4-3-329, Bank Street
Hyderabad-500195
Ph: 24756967/24756400

Dedicated

This book is dedicated to a yogi
MASTER MAHA SINGH
who mended relations and excelled in each role he lived
SON | BROTHER | FRIEND | HUSBAND | FATHER |
FATHER-IN-LAW | TEACHER | FARMER | CITIZEN | DEVOTEE
the most upright, conscientious, and able man I know
We miss you in every possible way papa.

Acknowledgements

To write a book, one need to be in a certain state of mind where one is secure from inside so that he can work with single minded focus.

A guru helps you be in that state. We want to thank our ideological and spiritual gurus.

Time spent on this book was the time stolen from the family and friends. Wish to thank them all.

We also wish to thank each other, but that would be tantamount to one half of the body thanking the other half for supporting it. The body does not function that way.

The Gang-of-kids deserves a special mention, starting from the oldest to the youngest, Sanjay, Shaalu, Jyoti, Roopal, Himanshu, Saurabh, Ritu, Vivek, Umesh, Pearl, Ritvik, Ritambhara, Kiaan, Moksha and Kaina. You guys are awesome.

Book writing is like a yajna, it cannot be complete without the blessings of the elders. Thanks Mom & Dad.

Preface

As a programming language, C is lightweight, powerful and full of exciting features. In an interview, you are not expected to use built-in functionality available in the language library. For example, if an interviewer asks you to sort an array, he does not want you to write

```
int arr[] = {2, 5, 3, 1, 4, 9, 0, 8, 7, 6};
std::sort(arr, arr+10);
```

He expect you to write the complete algorithm from scratch. Similarly, the problem to compute `100!` becomes amazingly easy if you are using a language like Python where variables can store as large a number as you want. The interviewer does not want you to write a simple code to compute factorial of a number, he may be interested in seeing how you handle a situation when the numbers become larger than the range of a data type. In a coding interview, you are not expected to use many built-in features of a programming language.

In a Coding Interview, the interviewer does not just want you to be a user of the programming language, you should think like the creators of the language. Java does not have pointers, but a Java programmer should also know about memory leaks and dangling pointers, because interviewer may be interested in knowing how will you create your own *Garbage Collector*.

Coding in a high-level language comes with some overhead of writing extra code to define class and, complicated function. When you are writing code with the pen in a time-critical interview, C language comes in handy.

Even when I was working on Android and coding in Java, I preferred C language to code the interview questions in my Microsoft interview.

Memory model of C is much simpler and we can easily run-thru the code without getting into the complexity of template libraries and threads.

One more reason why many use C language in interviews is to avoid any miscommunication with the interviewer. If interviewer is a person with knowledge in Java and you are coding in C#, it may take him some time to get to the language syntaxes. C is a language that is known to almost every programmer, making it a common language of technical communication in interviews.

This book is not a tutorial guide for absolute non-programmers. You must have written some programs (may be simple ones) to better comprehend it. We believe, students and professionals will read it multiple time to get an insight into language internals and write error-free codes.

Table of Contents

Preface v

1. The Underlay 1
  Question 1. 1: What is C89, C90, C99, and C11?...........................1
    K & R Method: 1
    ANSI C Method: 2
  Question 1. 2: What are the different stages in
  compilation process of a C language program?............................4
    Pre-processing 5
    Compiling...11
    Assembly 14
    Linking 14
  Question 1. 3: How is a C language program executed?...............16
    Code segment 17
    Data Segment 18
    Stack Segment 18
    Heap Segment 19
  Question 1. 4: What is static and dynamic linking? 26
    Static linking 26
    Dynamic Linking 26
  Question 1. 5: What is Undefined behaviour, Unspecified
  behaviour and Implementation-defined behaviour? 27
  Question 1. 6: What is the maximum value of
  integer data type in C language?..30

Question 1. 7: What are the different data types?..............................32

Question 1. 8: What are literals in C language? 33

Question 1. 9: What is the output of the following code? 35

Question 1. 10: What are storage classes in C? 37

    Automatic...37

    Register..38

    Global..38

    Static...39

Question 1. 11: Why does the following code print the
values mentioned in the comments for variables ivar? 40

Question 1. 12: What is the output of the following code? 40

Question 1. 13: Which of the following programs
will take less time to execute and why?...42

Question 1. 14: What is prototyping and what are
extern variables ?..43

Question 1. 15: What are Type Qualifiers ?.....................................45

    volatile 45

    Const...46

    Restrict 46

Question 1. 16: What are the signatures of printf
and scanf functions?..46

Question 1. 17: What is the difference between
typedef and #define ? 48

    Pre-processor versus Compiler...48

    Macro v/s type alias 49

Question 1. 18: What are identifiers and why we cannot have an
identifier name starting with number?...50

2. Operators And Statements...53

Question 2. 1: Give the list of all operators
available in C?...53

Question 2. 2: How does the below array change after following operations?......................64

Question 2. 3: What is the output of Code 2.2?......................65

Question 2. 4: What is a NULL statement and where is it used?......................66

Question 2. 5: What is conditional and unconditional branching. 69

Question 2. 6: What is Dangling-Else problem?......................77

Question 2. 7: What are the different looping structures in C language?......................78

    While Loop......................78

    For Loop......................80

    Do-While Loop 81

Question 2. 8: Which of the following two codes take more time? 82

    Row-Major......................84

    Column-Major 84

Question 2. 9: How are the following two codes different? 84

Question 2. 10: Can we rewrite a for loop as while loop without distorting the logic?......................85

Question 2. 11: What is the output of following code? 86

Question 2. 12: While comparing a variable with a constant (literal), which of the two comparison should be used ?......................86

3. Pointers And Memory......................88

Question 3. 1: What is lvalue and rvalue?......................88

Question 3. 2: What are pointers? How do we use them in C?......................91

    Pointer Operators 91

Question 3. 3: Which operations can be performed on pointers?......................94

Question 3. 4: What are void pointers? 96

Question 3. 5: What is Big-Endian versus Little Endian? 97

Big Endian 98

Little Endian 98

Which one is better: 99

Question 3. 6: What is a memory leak and what
are dangling pointers? 100

Memory leak..100

Dangling pointers: 103

1. uninitialized locals 103

2. Pointing to out-of-scope variables 103

3. Explicitly deallocating memory. 104

4. Side effect of deallocating memory 104

5. Returning address of a local variable on stack. 104

Question 3. 7: How do you swap two variables
without using third variable? 105

Method-1: Using XOR Method 106

Method-2: Add-subtract method 106

Question 3. 8: What is a NULL Pointer? 107

Question 3. 9: What are near, far and huge pointers? 108

Question 3. 10: How does free() function know
the size of memory to be deallocated? 109

Question 3. 11: What is the difference between
malloc, and calloc functions? 109

1. Signature 109

2. Initialization 110

3. Faster 110

Question 3. 12: What is the use of realloc function? 110

Question 3. 13: Write a function to check if the stack
is growing forward or backward? 111

Question 3. 14: Write code that accepts a string and
print the following pattern; If string is "RAM",
then output should be 113

4. Advanced Data Types 116

Question 4. 1: How will you define a generic array
that can hold all kinds of data? 116

Question 4. 2: What will happen if we partially
initialize an array? 117

Question 4. 3: How do you allocate array on heap? 118

    2-dimensional array: 121

    N-dim Array..123

    Deallocating 1-dimensional array 123

    Deallocating 2-dimensional Array................................124

    Deallocating N-dimensional array................................124

Question 4. 4: Is array name a pointer to type or
a pointer to array? 125

Question 4. 5: What are function pointers and
how can they be used? 126

    Type of a function..126

    Complicated declarations 128

Question 4. 6: Can we declare array of any type?..............129

Question 4. 7: Can we have a variable length array? 129

Question 4. 8: How do we pass 2-dim arrays to function? 130

Question 4. 9: How is strlen different from sizeof? 131

Question 4. 10: Can I use sizeof on array parameters?.....................133

Question 4. 11: Implement strcpy function.......................133

Question 4. 12: Write a function to swap two strings.....................133

Question 4. 13: What is wrong in Code 4.6 below? 135

Question 4. 14: How do you find the size of a
structure type without using sizeof operator on
the structure (you can apply sizeof on individual fields)? 136

Question 4. 15: Can we have a structure field of
the same struct type like below? 138

Question 4. 16: What are dynamic arrays? 139

    Static sized arrays 139

Variable length arrays..140
Dynamic Arrays..140

5. Functions And File Handling 142
Question 5. 1: What is the difference between
'infinite loop' and 'infinite recursion'?..................................142
Question 5. 2: Print Hello n times without using a loop?............143
Question 5. 3: What are static functions in C?.........................144
Question 5. 4: How can a function return multiple values? 144
Question 5. 5: What is the output of below printf function?.........146
Question 5. 6: What is the signature of main function? 146
Question 5. 7: How can we change pointers passed
to function as parameters? 147
Question 5. 8: What is pass-by-value and pass-by-reference? 151
Question 5. 9: What is a stream? 152

6. Bit Twiddling 155
Question 6. 1: What is masking and how is it used? 155
Question 6. 2: What is the difference between
logical-NOT and bitwise-NOT operators?................................157
Question 6. 3: Write a function that returns nth
bit in binary representation of an integral................................157
Question 6. 4: Get lowest set bit of a number..........................158
Question 6. 5: Reset the lowest set bit of a number.
If number is 00001010 then result should be 00001000..............158
Question 6. 6: How do you check if a number is
power of two or not? 4, 8, 1024 etc. are powers
of two, 6, 40, 95 etc. are not...159
Method-1: Take log base-2..159
Method-2: Keep dividing by 2..159
Method-3: Use Bitwise operators 160

Question 6. 7: Count set bits in an integer............................160

Question 6. 8: Add two numbers without using
arithmetic operator...161

Question 6. 9: Given an unsigned int n, find
the smallest integer greater than or equal to n
which is a power of 2. For example:.......................................162

Question 6. 10: Given two unsigned integers,
how can you find greater and smaller of the two
without comparing them?...162

Question 6. 11: Write a function to compute xn..................163

    Method-1: Brute Force - O(n) time..................................163

    Method-2: Optimal Solution - O(lg(n)) time.................164

Question 6. 12: Computing 2n..165

Question 6. 13: Check for Odd-Even...................................166

Question 6. 14: Find the missing number............................167

Question 6. 15: All elements in an integer array are
repeating even number of times, except for one
which is repeating odd number of times. Find the number
repeating odd number of times...169

Question 6. 16: Find the missing and repeating number. 170

    Method-1: Using Sorting...170

    Solution-2: Using Hashing..170

    Solution-3: Using XOR...171

Question 6. 17: Function randomBit() is a Random
number generator that generates 0 or 1 with equal probability.
Write a function using randomBit(), that generate 0 and 1
with 25% and 75% probability respectively. 173

7. Left Over..174

Question 7. 1: Is it better to use global variable or pass
parameters to function? 174

Question 7. 2: What are the common sources of error
in C language? 176

1. Non-terminated comment: 176

2. Faulty expressions:...176

3. Order of evaluation 177

4. Accidental placement of semicolon or missing braces............177

5. De-Referencing dangling pointers or wrong pointer 178

6. Not checking pointer parameters against NULL...................178

7. Integer division 179

8. Using strict equality with floating points 180

9. Returning garbage from a function. 181

10. High nested indentation. 181

11. Choose meaningful variable names....................................182

12. Do not ignore compiler warnings 182

Question 7. 3: How to print "Hello World" without
using any semicolon? 182

Question 7. 4: Which of the two loops will run faster? 184

Question 7. 5: How is const qualifier used in C language? 184

Question 7. 6: What is the output of following program? 186

Question 7. 7: If ptr is a pointer to array, then what is
the difference between ++*ptr and *ptr++? 186

Question 7. 8: How will you sort an array of Students
on marks field? Structure of Student is defined as follows:..............187

Question 7. 9: What are assertions in C language?...........................190

Question 7. 10: What is the purpose of fork()? 191

How do we know whether we are in parent or
child process? 193

1.

THE UNDERLAY

Question 1. 1: What is C89, C90, C99, and C11?

There were very few operating systems back in 1970s whose kernel was implemented in a language other than Assembly. One of the motivations behind developing C language was to rewrite Unix operating system in a high-level language.

Prior to 1989, the version of C that served as informal standard was called K&R C (for *Kernighan* and *Ritchie*). In 1989, standard of C was ratified by **American National Standard Institute** (**ANSI**) and this standard was called ANSI C, Standard C or just **C89**.

One year later in 1990, this ANSI standard was adopted by ISO, International Standard Organization, and is sometimes called **C90** or ISO C. There are many differences between K&R C and ANSI C. Consider the way of declaring prototypes in these two forms.

K & R Method:

```
#include <stdio.h>
void printTriangle();
int main()
{
   int lines = 5, printChar='*';
   printTriangle(lines, printChar);
}


void printTriangle(numLine, printChar)
int numLine;
char printChar;
{
   int count, inCount;
   for(count=1; count<= numLine; count++)
   {
     for(inCount=1;inCount<=count; inCount++)
       printf("%c ", printChar);
```

```
        printf("\n");
    }
}
```

Code 1.1

ANSI C Method:

```
#include <stdio.h>
void printTriangle(int, char);
int main()
{
    int lines = 5, printChar='*';
    printTriangle(lines, printChar);
}

void printTriangle(int numLine, char printChar)
{
    int count, inCount;
    for(count=1; count<=numLine; count++)
    {
        for(inCount=1;inCount<=count; inCount++)
            printf("%c ", printChar);
        printf("\n");
    }
}
```

Code 1.2

Both programs will compile and execute with the following output:

```
*
* *
* * *
* * * *
* * * * *
```

But, observe the difference in function prototypes. In K&R method only function-name is important whereas ANSI standard also requires parameter list to be present. Macro __STDC__ is used to split code for separate compilation for K&R C and ANSI C.

```
#if __STDC__
```

```
  /* CODE CONFIRMING ANSI C */
#else
  /* CODE CONFIRMING K&R C */
#endif
```

In 1999, a new standard, **C99** came. It was much more strict and had many big-ticket changes like variable length arrays, support for single-line comment, new data types like `Complex`, `long` and an explicit `bool`.

So, the following code is NOT error in C language because array-length can be a variable:

```
int n = 10;
int arr[n]; // VARIABLE LENGTH ARRAY
```

For most part, C99 is backward compatible with C90. All C compilers provide support for most of the features of C99. Microsoft has been slow in updating its compiler with the latest C standards.

Standard mandates that implementations (compilers) should define macro `__STDC_VERSION__` to integer constant `199901L` in C99. It can be used as a check to see if compiler supports C99.

```
#if __STDC_VERSION__ == 199901L
    // C99 SUPPORT
#endif
```

C11 is the standard of C language that was published in 2011. One of the biggest features added in this new standard is header `threads.h` that adds multi-threading support (thread support is optional, check macro `__STDC_NO_THREADS__`) in addition to other features like static assertions and unicode support. C11 standard mandates implementations to define `__STDC_VERSION__` to integer constant `201112L` that can be used as a check to see if compiler supports C11.

```
#if __STDC_VERSION__ >= 201112L
    // C11 SUPPORT
#endif
```

As we are writing this book, in September 2017, C11 is the latest standard and Clang and GCC are most updated with the latest standard.

Question 1. 2: What are the different stages in the compilation process of a C language program?

We are using `gcc` to demonstrate the process (may not be exactly same for other compilers). It all starts with writing code in a source code file. To illustrate the process, consider the following program in file `myfirst.c`:

```
#include <stdio.h>

/* MACRO TO ADD TWO NUMBERS */
#define SUM(X,Y)  (X)+(Y)

int main(void)
{
   int x, y;

   printf("ENTER VALUES : ");    // READING VALUES
   scanf("%d%d", &x, &y);

   printf("SUM IS %d", SUM(x,y));   // PRINTING SUM
   return 0;
}
```

Code 1.3

Code 1.3 reads two integers and print their sum. For demonstration, we are using a macro to compute the actual sum. Compile this source code using the following commands (we are using gcc on MAC OS):

```
$ gcc myfirst.c
```

This command creates an executable with the name `a.out`. Now run this executable:

```
$ ./a.out
```

For executable to have some other name, use `-o` in the `gcc` command:.

```
$ gcc myfirst.c -o myfirst
$ ./myfirst
```

The above `gcc` command took our source code thru four steps before generating the final executable. The word *compilation* is used to represent this journey of a piece of code from source code (`.c` file) to executable (`.exe` on Windows). This journey has the following four stages:

1. Pre-processing
2. Compiling
3. Assembly
4. Linking

This may look like a recursive definition because, entire process, involving these four steps is also called compilation. Meaning of the word compilation will be clear from the context.
Let us look into each of these stages in detail.

Pre-processing

In this phase, essentially the following two things happen:
1. Evaluation of pre-processor directives (Macro Substitution, In-line Expansion, Conditional compilation, and so on.)
2. Stripping comments and extra white space.

In the overall compilation process, tokens are generated twice. Once during the pre-processing and then during compilation. Pre-processor looks for directive-tokens (starting with #) and take action against each token it can find. Pre-processor directives are different from statements in many ways:
✓ They are always preceded by a pound (#) sign (*This sign indicates that rest of the line is a pre-processor directive. We may precede pound by spaces but it is not common practice to indent pre-processor directives*)
✓ Statements are terminated by a semicolon but no semicolon is expected at the end of a directive.
✓ Directives are handled by the pre-processor, whereas statements are handled in the compilation phase.
✓ A macro cannot run into multiple lines by default. To write a multi-line macro, put slash (\) character at end of the line as shown in the following code snippet:

```
#define SWAP(X, Y, _T) { _T _t;  \
                _t = X;  \
                X = Y;   \
                Y = _t;}
```

Pre-processor consider next line as part of same macro only if the current line has a slash in the end.

✓ You cannot have more than one directives in a single line, but more than one statement in a single line (separated by semicolons) is possible. In fact, entire program (except directives) can be written in one line.

✓ Scope rule does not apply to the pre-processor directives. They come into effect when they are encountered and remain in effect going forward. For example:

```
#define MY_CONST 10
int main(){
  int x = 10;
  {
    int x = 5;
    printf("First : %d - %d\n", MY_CONST, x);

    #define MY_CONST 20
  }
  printf("Second : %d - %d\n", MY_CONST, x);
}
```

Output:
```
First : 10 - 5
Second : 20 - 10
```

Earlier definition of MY_CONST is overwritten when new definition is found.

Following is list of pre-processor directives available in C:

- # : null directive, has no effect.
- #include : Include a file.
- #define : Define a macro.
- #undef : Undefine a macro.
- #if, #ifdef, #ifndef, #elif, #else, #endif:

For conditional compilation

- #line : To control error reporting
- #error : To force an error message.
- #pragma : For implementation-dependent controls.

Null directive is just to say that, a single # without anything following it is not an error, though it does not serve any purpose.

When pre-processor encounters a directive, it perform the corresponding action and delete the directive from the source file. The file that reaches the next phase does not have any directives in it.

`#include` directive has two forms (differing in locations where file with name `filename` is searched)

✔ `#include <filename>`
✔ `#include "filename"`

Pre-processor replace `include` directive with contents of file specified in the directive, also expanding nested includes. Included files are also compiled along with file in which they are included, and the errors in included file (if any) are also reported as part of the compilation process.

Macro is the name given to a code fragment. Where ever this name is present in the file, pre-processor replace it with contents of the macro. There are two kinds of macro definitions, first one looks like a constant definition and second resembles function definition. For the following two macros:

```
#define PI 3.14
#define SUM(X,Y) X+Y
```

Pre-processor will replace `PI` with `3.14`, `SUM(2,3)` with `2+3` and `SUM(2.5,3.4)` with `2.5+3.4` in the following `printf` statement:

```
printf("%d %lf %lf", SUM(2,3), PI, SUM(2.5,3.4));
```

Same macro is used to compute sum of two integers and sum of two doubles. Unlike functions, macros are generic and can be called with different types of parameters.

A macro can be redefined. If `RATE` is `10` in first part of program and `20` in second part, macro name `RATE` can be redefined as shown in the following code:

```
#define RATE 10
    ... ...
    ... ... // RATE REPLACED WITH 10 HERE
#define RATE 20
```

```
... ...
... ... // RATE REPLACED WITH 20 HERE
```

A common use of macro is to take platform specific action based on the macros defined for the platform. If MACHINTOSH is a macro, defined only on MAC machines and we have separate code for MAC and PC, then the following code compiles separate function calls for these platform:

```
#ifdef MACHINTOSH
  myFunc_MAC();
#else
  myFunc_PC();
#endif
```

The most rampant use of macro definitions is to avoid multiple inclusion of header files. Every header file (.h) is guarded using macros to handle multiple inclusion.

Macros also give performance advantage by expanding the code inline before compilation, thus avoiding any run-time execution overhead (like function call). But macros are more prone to errors because the body of a macro is replaced and not executed like a function. Consider the following macro to compute the square of a number:

```
#define SQR(X) X*X
```

Results of this macro for various different parameters are as follows:

Call	Replaced text	Result
SQR(5)	5*5	25
SQR(2+3)	2+3*2+3	11
SQR(6)	6*6	36
SQR(1+2+3)	1+2+3*1+2+3	11

It works fine when it's called for singular values like 5 or 6 but fails when called for expressions. Expectation from SQR(2+3) is to give square of 5 and not 11.

This is because macros do not have any computing power; they just do a blind replacement. In SQR, whatever is there between parenthesis is taken as X and macro is replaced with X*X.

This macro can be improved using parentheses in the definition.

```
#define SQR(X) (X)*(X)
```

Now `SQR(1+2+3)` will get replaced with `(1+2+3)*(1+2+3)`, which gives the expected result, `36`. Looks like we have written a fool-proof macro.

Well, Yes and No.

Yes, because this macro cannot be improved further, and No because it is still not error-free. A call like `SQR(x++)` will fail the macro. The replaced text is `(x++)*(x++)` and the answer is undefined (updating a variable more than once in a single expression).

These are the side effects of macros which all C-programmers must understand and practice good coding guidelines, like, *"Do not apply increment/ decrement operator in macro call"*. If you want to increment, then you must explicitly define the operation as one of the following:

```
// TO INCREMENT BEFORE        // TO INCREMENT AFTER
x++;                          SQR(x);
SQR(x);                       x++;
```

String literals are treated as a single token by both pre-processor and compiler, pre-processor do not search for macro names inside them. Take a look at the following code:

```
#define MY_NAME Ritambhara
int main(){
    printf("%s", "MY_NAME");
}
```

Prints `MY_NAME` as output. However, a macro can represent a string, as shown in the following code:

```
#define MAIN   int main()
#define Begin  {
#define End    }
#define MSG    "Hello World"
#define PRINT(X) printf("%s", X);

MAIN
Begin
    PRINT(MSG);
End
```

While compiling in gcc, -E flag prints output of pre-processor to console. -save-temps option instructs compiler to store these temporary intermediate files used by gcc in current directory. Compile program in Code 1.3 using the following command:

```
$ gcc -save-temps myfirst.c -o myfirst
```

This command creates some extra files along with executable myfirst. Pre-processed output is stored in file with .i extension. In this case, it is myfirst.i. Following are some parts of this file:

```
# 1 "myfirst.c"
# 1 "<built-in>" 1
... ... ...
... ... ...
extern FILE *__stdinp;
extern FILE *__stdoutp;
extern FILE *__stderrp;
... ... ...
... ... ...
FILE *fopen(const char * restrict __filename, const
          char * restrict __mode) __asm("_" "fopen" );
int fputc(int, FILE *);
... ... ...
... ... ...
int getc(FILE *);
int getchar(void);
char *gets(char *);
void perror(const char *);
int printf(const char * restrict, ...)
    __attribute__((__format__ (__printf__, 1, 2)));
int putc(int, FILE *);
int putchar(int);
... ... ...
... ... ...
int main(void)
{
  int x, y;

  printf("ENTER VALUES : ");
  scanf("%d%d", &x, &y);

  printf("SUM IS %d", (x)+(y));
  return 0;
}
```

The `printf` statement contains `(x)+(y)` directly and all directives including the macro definitions are deleted. Also, comments in the original file are gone and entire content of `stdio.h` file is added in place of `#include` directive. If we search the file, `stdio.h`, we will find declaration of `printf` function.

```
int printf(const char * restrict, ...)
    __attribute__((__format__(__printf__,1, 2)));
```

Note: *Above code is only the declaration and not the definition.*

Compiling

This stage takes the output of pre-processing (`myfirst.i`) as an input, compile it for syntax and semantics correctness and produce an intermediate compiled output, `myfirst.s` which has assembly code. If we do not have the code, but have the `.i` file, we may use the following command:

```
$ gcc -S myfirst.i
```

Option `-S` is used to convert pre-processed code to assembly language. This process has the following routines:

1. **Lexical Analysis:** All the statements in a C program are further divided into tokens. A Token is a sequence of the characters that represent a lexical unit (keywords, operators, identifiers, constant, separator, and so on.). For the following code:

```
if(x < 10)
   x = x - 5;
else
   x = x + 5;
```

Lexical analyser generates the following tokens:
- **Keywords:** `if` `else`
- **Identifiers:** `x`
- **Constants:** `5`, `10`
- **Operators:** `<` `=` `-` `+`
- **Others:** `(` `)` `;`

Once a token is generated, entry of the corresponding identifier is added into the **Symbol table**. Every identifier gets an ID in the symbol table. Let us assume that ID of x is `ID_1`.

2. **Syntax Analysis:** It is also called parsing. Syntax analyser (also called parser) checks for language syntax and generate parse tree for the statements. Parse tree for `x=5+10;` is shown in Figure 1.1.

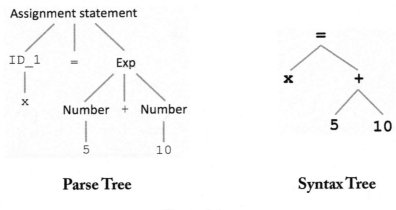

Parse Tree   **Syntax Tree**

Figure 1.1

A parse tree represents the syntactic structure of a statement according to the grammar of C language. Syntax tree is more compressed representation of parse tree where operators are at non-leaf nodes and operands are at leaf.

If syntax is not as per grammar rules of language, error is generated. Error generated at this stage is called parsing error.

3. **Semantic Analysis:** Checks for type mismatch and semantic consistency. If a variable is declared as float and modulus operator is used on that variable, then it is a semantic error.

First three phases are independent of platform and machine. The output of these operations change only when we change the language version. They are jointly called front-end operations.

4. **Intermediate Code Generation:** This creates a logical separation between machine-dependent phase and source-dependent phase by producing an intermediate representation for source code in the form

of, postfix notation, thread address code, syntax tree, and so on. Next two steps have heavy dependency on the target machine.

5. **Code Optimization:** It gets the intermediate code and produces optimized intermediate code as output. The output code results in faster running machine code. There are multiple optimizations that can be performed on the code by compiler:
   - Loop unrolling
   - Removing unwanted temporary variables
   - Deduction and removal of dead code
   - Inline expansion of smaller functions
   - Unfolding recursion

6. **Code Generation:** Final phase of the compilation process. Gets input from code optimization phase and generate code for the target machine. Output of this phase may depend on the CPU architecture of target device. Intermediate instructions are translated into a sequence of machine instructions that perform the same task.

In all these steps, compiler make use of Symbol table and Error handling module.

Symbol table is usually implemented as a Hash tables to keep track of identifiers. It stores all information (name, type, scope) about identifiers used in the program. Whenever an identifier is detected in any phase, it is stored in the symbol table.

Error handling module is used for reporting and recovery of errors that occur in each stage of compilation. Goal is to report the presence of each error clearly and accurately. This module should recover from each error really fast to detect subsequent errors and add minimal overhead to compilation process.

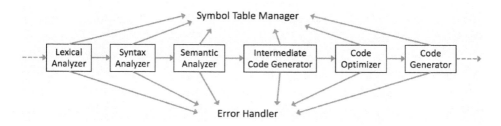

Figure 1.2

Assembly

The output of the compiling phase is input of assembly phase. Assembler takes `myfirst.s` as an input, interpret the assembly language code and convert it to machine language object file, `myfirst.o`.

Calls to external functions like `printf` are not resolved at this stage. There are many formats for object file, popular ones being `a.out` (Original file format for Unix), (**Executable and Linking Format (ELF)**, used on many modern Unix systems) and **Common Object-File format (COFF)**.

Object file has sections to hold executable code, data, dynamic linking information, debugging data, symbol tables, relocation information, comments, string tables, and notes.

Some sections are used while loading the executable, some sections provide information needed in building of executable while others are used only in linking the object files.

Assembling to machine code remove traces of labels from code, the object file format keep them in different places using symbol table that contains a list of names and their offsets in text and data segments.

Different sections are discussed in detail in *Question 1.3*. You can also make a stand alone call to the assembler if you have `.s` file

```
$ as myfirst.s -o myfirst.o
```

Object file contains executable code of our program with the undefined reference to the external functions like `printf` and `scanf`.

Linking

This is the last stage in compilation process. It takes output of previous phase as input and generate the final executable.

The file generated in the previous phase, `myfirst.o`, does not have definition of functions like `printf` and `scanf`. A place-holder was kept at the place of a function call to be replaced by the linker with actual function call in this phase of linking.

While linking, definitions of function like `printf` are resolved and actual addresses of these functions are plugged in. linker also adds some extra code in the program executable. This extra code is required during the execution. Operating system hands over control to this code. This code sets up the running environment like passing command line arguments to `main` function, passing environment variables and calling the `main` function.

If you look at the size of object file created by the assembler and size of executable created by the linker, you can see the difference.

```
$ size myfirst.o
__TEXT   __DATA   __OBJC   others   dec   hex
187          0        0       32         219   db

$ size myfirst
__TEXT   __DATA   __OBJC   others       dec          hex
4096      4096      0    4294971392   4294979584   100003000
```

Part of it is also because of standard code added by the linker. The link command executed by the linker is complex and involves physical path to libraries on the system. ld is link command, and it is similar (not same) to the following:

```
$ ld -dynamic-linker /lib64/ld-linux-x86-64.so.2
   ... ... ... -lgcc ... ... ... -o myfirst
```

It is not the complete command, please refer ld command on your system. *Figure 1.3* shows the complete process:

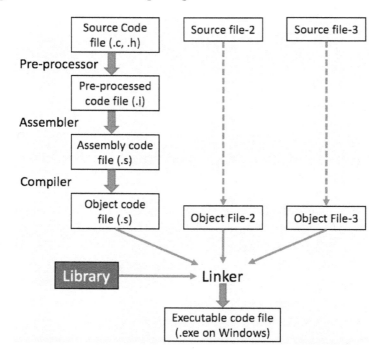

Figure 1.3

It is the linker that enables separate compilation of different modules into object files and then combine them into one executable.

Different object files has references to each other's code and data at different locations (like a call to printf inside object file myfirst.o). These references are combined during link-time. After linking object files together, linker use relocation records to find all addresses that need to be filled in.

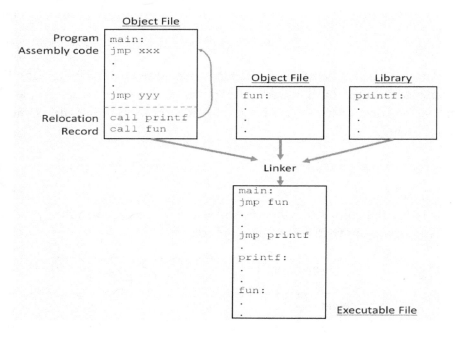

Figure 1.4

Question 1. 3: How is a C language program executed?

After compiling and linking, binary executable of C language program gets generated (.exe on windows). When this binary is actually executing (running) it is called a **process** (*Most IDEs compile, link and execute program on a single button click. But internally all these steps are performed*).

While executing, a process is first loaded into the memory (RAM). Area of memory where the process is loaded is called **process address space**. Figure 1.5 shows broad layout of process address space (*The actual layout may* *differ for operating system/program, ISO standard does not talk about Stack or other areas, it is largely an implementation thing. But the figure is very close to how it is on most systems).*

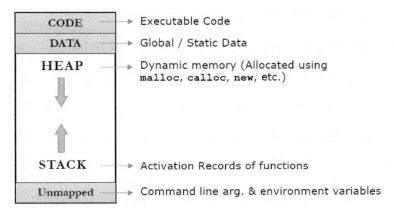

Figure 1.5

This memory is allocated to process by operating system. The process address space is divided in the following segments:

1. Code segment (or Text segment)
2. Data segment
3. Stack segment
4. Heap segment

Let us discuss these segments one by one.

Code segment

- ✓ This segment contains machine code (in the form of executable instructions) of compiled program.
- ✓ It is read-only and cannot be changed when program is executing.
- ✓ Size of code segment is fixed during the load time.
- ✓ May be shareable, so that only a single copy is in the memory for different executing programs (*Sharable code is out of scope of this book*).
- ✓ On embedded systems, the code segment is written in ROM.

Data Segment

- ✓ All global and static variables are allocated memory in this area.
- ✓ Memory in this segment is allocated when the program is loading (before actual execution). That's why global and static variables are also called **load-time variables**.
- ✓ All load-time variables (global and static), are initialized at the load-time. If no initial value is given for a variable, then it is initialized with the zero of its type (Zero of int data type is 0. Zero of pointer data type is NULL).
- ✓ Internally, this segment is divided into two areas initialized and uninitialized (bss segment). If initial value of a variable is given, it goes in the initialized data area, else it goes in the uninitialized data area.

  All uninitialized variables are then initialized with zeros. This is the reason why they are stored separately within the data segment, so that entire memory can be memset to zero in a single operation.

- ✓ After loading, the initialized and uninitialized data segments are indistinguishable.
- ✓ Size of data segment is fixed at load time and does not change while program is executing.

Stack Segment

Stack segment contains **Activation Records** (also called Stack Frames) of all active functions. An active function is a function that is currently under call. Consider the following Code 1.4:

```
int main(){
   fun1();
}
void fun1(){
   fun2();
}
void fun2(){
}
void fun3(){
   // NEVER CALLED
}
```

Code 1.4

When main function is called, it is the only active function. Then main calls fun1, at this point fun1 is executing but both main and fun1 are active. When fun1 calls fun2, then the execution is in fun2, but the main, fun1 and fun2 are all active and have their activation records are present in the Stack.

When function fun2 returns, activation record of fun2 is popped from the Stack and execution returns in fun1. At this point, main and fun1 are active and have their activation records in Stack.

The function fun3 is never active because it is never called and hence its activation record never gets created on the Stack.

- ✓ When a function is called, its Activation Record is created and pushed on the top of stack.
- ✓ When a function returns, the corresponding Activation Record is popped from the Stack.
- ✓ Size of Stack keeps changing while the program is executing, as the number of active functions keep changing.
- ✓ Non-static local variables of a function are allocated memory in Activation Record of that function when it is active.
- ✓ Variables allocated memory on Stack are not initialized by default. If initial value of a variable is not given, then it is not initialized and its value will be garbage (this is different from load-time variables allocated memory in Data Segment).
- ✓ Activation record also contains other information required in function execution.
- ✓ **Stack Pointer (SP)** keeps track of the top of Stack.
- ✓ Function whose Activation Record is at the top of Stack, is the one that is executing currently. Function whose activation record is in the Stack, but not at the top, is active but not executing.
- ✓ If a function is recursive then multiple activation records of the same function is present in the Stack.

Heap Segment

- ✓ When we allocate memory at run time using malloc(), calloc(), and realloc() in C language (new and new[] in C++), then that memory is allocated on Heap. It is also called **dynamic memory** or **run-time memory**.

✓ In C language, we cannot initialize the memory allocated on Heap. In C++, if we use `new` operator to allocate memory, then we can initialize it using constructors.

✓ Memory allocated on heap does not have a name (unlike Data and Stack segments). The only way to access this memory is via pointers pointing to it. If we lose address of this memory, there is no way to access it and such a memory will become **memory leak**. It is one of the largest sources of error in C/C++ programming.

✓ Both Heap and Stack segment shares a common area and grows toward each other.

After compilation and linking, the executable code (in machine language) gets generated. The first thing that happens when this executable code is executed is that it is loaded in the memory. **Loading** has the following steps:

✓ **Code goes in code area.** Code is in the form of binary machine instructions and **Instruction Pointer** (**IP**) holds the address of current instruction being executed.

✓ **Global and static variables are allocated memory in the data area**. Data area has two sub-parts, Initialized and Uninitialized data area, if initial value of a variable is given by us, it gets allocated in the Initialized data area, else memory to the variable is allocated in the un-initialized data area and it is initialized with zero.

✓ **Global and static variables are initialized**. If we have given the initial value explicitly, then variables are initialized with that value, otherwise they are initialized with zeros of their data types.

```
int x = 5; // initialized with 5
int y;     // initialized with 0
```

After these steps, we say that *the program is loaded*. Once the loading is complete, the `main` function is called and actual execution of the program begins. Read the entire program given in Code 1.5 carefully:

```
// Go in data area at load time. Initialized with 0.
int total;

/** Code (machine instructions) of function goes in
 * code area. When this function is called, then
```

```
 * Activation Record of the function is created on
 * Stack.
 */
int square(int x){
  // x goes in Activation Record of this function.
  return x*x;
}

/** Code of function goes in the code area. When this
 * function is called (at run-time), its AR gets
 * created on Stack and memory to non-static local
 * variables (x and y) is allocated in that AR.
 * count, being a static variable, is allocated in
 * data area at load time.
 */
int squareOfSum(int x, int y){
  static int count = 0; // Load-time var
  printf("Fun called %d times", ++count);
  return square(x+y);
}

/** Code goes in code area. When main is called, its
 * activation record gets created on Stack and memory
 * to non-static local variables (a and b) is
 * allocated in that Activation Record.
 */
int main(){
  int a=4, b=2;
  total = squareOfSum(a, b);
  printf("Square of Sum = %d",total);
}
```

Code 1.5

This program computes $(a+b)^2$ and print the result. To keep it simple, we are using the hard-coded values 4 and 2 for a and b respectively. The function squareOfSum also keeps a count of how many times it is called in a static variable count, and print this count every time it is called.

Code 1.5 may not be the best implementation, but it serves our purpose. Read the code again, especially the comments before each function and make sure that you understand everything.

After compilation and linking the executable of the program gets generated and when this executable is run, the first thing that happens is that, this executable is loaded in the memory (RAM). At this point the main function is not yet called and the memory looks like Figure 1.6:

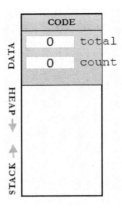

Figure 1.6

After loading is complete, main function is called. Whenever a function is called, its Activation Record is created and pushed in the Stack. The AR has the following:

✓ Local (non-static) variables of a function (a and b for main).
✓ Other things stored in the Activation Record.

In the diagrams, we are only showing the non-static local variables in Activation Records. After main function is called, the memory looks as shown in Figure 1.7.

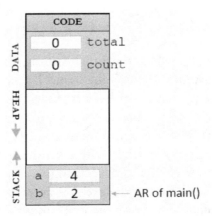

Figure 1.7

At any time, the point of execution (Instruction Pointer) is in the function whose AR is at the top of Stack. Let us understand what all happens internally when a function is called by another function.

When a function is called:

1. State (register values, Instruction Pointer value, and so on.) of calling function is saved in the memory. Value of local variables of a function under execution are stored in the AR of the function in the stack are of memory. But registers may also store copy of some of these values. The state of registers may also be saved.

2. Activation record of the called function is created. Local variables (non-static) of the called function are allocated memory inside the AR.

3. Instruction pointer (IP register) moves to the first executable instruction of called function.

4. Execution of the called function begins.

Similarly, when the called function returns back (to the calling function), following work is done:

1. Return value of the function is stored in some register.

2. AR of the called function is popped from the memory (Stack size is reduced and freed memory gets added to the free pool, which can be used by either the stack or heap).

3. State of the calling function is restored back to what it was before the function call (Point-1 in function call process above).

4. Instruction pointer moves back to the instruction of the calling function, where it was before the function call was made (*This is conceptually similar to the* **Context Switch** *that happens in a mutiprocessing operating system when a process is pre-empted to execute another process and after some time control returns back to the first process and the first process starts executing from the same point where it was pre-empted*).

5. Value returned from called function is replaced at the point of call in calling function.

> A function call is a lot of overhead, in terms of time and memory.

One of the reasons behind the popularity of macros in C language (even after all the evil that they bring along) is this overhead in function call. Another was the type independence that macros bring (*In C++, both the benefits are given in the form of inline functions and templates and they are not error prone like macros*).

Some compilers optimize the performance by replacing function call with the entire code of the function during compilation, hence avoiding the actual function call overheads. This is called **Inline expansion**. In Code 1.5, the compiler may just put entire code of function `square` inside `squareOfSum` and remove the function call all together as shown code:

```
int squareOfSum(int x, int y){
   static int count = 0; // Load-time var
   printf("Fun called %d times", ++count);
   return (x+y) * (x+y);
}
```

Code 1.6

Recursive functions are very difficult to expand inline because compiler may not know the actual depth of function call at compile time.

Let us also see how memory looks like if we miss the terminating condition of a recursion. Code 1.7 is an example of infinite recursion.

```
int main(){
   int x = 0;
   x++;
   if(x<5){
     printf("Hello");
     main();
   }
}
```

Code 1.7

When this program is executed after compilation, it is first loaded into the memory and then the `main` function is called. At this point (after calling `main`) the memory looks as shown in the Figure 1.8. Code area has machine language code, Data area is empty because there is no load-time (global or static) variable. Stack has only one activation record of function `main`.

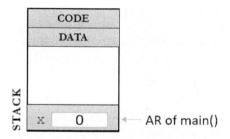

Figure 1.8

Initial value of x is 0, after increment x becomes 1, since x<5, the condition is true and main is called again. A new AR for this newly called main is created on the Memory Stack and this AR also has a local variable x that is different from the variable x in AR of previous call (see *Figure 1.9*). Value of this new x is again 0, and main is called again. Every time main is called, the value of x in the new activation record is 0.

Every instance of main is actually using a different x (from its own instance of AR).

Code 1.7 will continue to print "Hello", until a point comes when no space is left in the Stack to create the new AR. At this point, main cannot be called further and the program will crash.

An important thing to note is, the program will not print "Hello" infinitely. It is printed, until the memory stack overflows.

The size command, a GNU utility, reports the sizes of text, data, .bss segments, and total size for a file, we used it in *Question 1.2*.

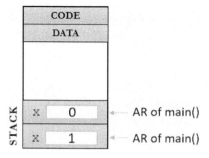

Figure 1.9

Question 1. 4: What is static and dynamic linking?

If more than one program is running and all of them are calling a standard C library function, say printf, each program may have a unique copy of this particular library as part of its executable within it. This may result in overall wastage of resources (memory to store same code at multiple places) and may degrade efficiency and performance. Since C library is common and the implementation of printf used by different programs is exactly same, it is better to have each program reference a single (common) instance of that library. This is implemented during linking process where some objects are linked during link-time (static linking) and some are left to be done during the run-time (dynamic linking).

Static linking

Statically linked means that the program is combined with the corresponding library at link time by the linker. The binding between program and library is fixed and known before the program executes. It also means that we cannot change this binding, unless we link the program again (creating new executable) with a different version of the library.

Programs that are linked statically are linked against archives of objects (libraries) that typically have the extension of .a, like the standard C library, libc.a.

It is good to link statically if you are not sure if correct version of library will be available at run-time or not. Linker extracts the actual code from the static library to build the final executable. If you want to test with a specific version of the library without installing that version, then also linking with that version statically is good. For gcc, -static option can be used during linking of the program.

```
gcc -static filename.c -o filename
```

The drawback of this technique is that the executable is bigger in size and hence take more time and memory to load. A demo on how to create and use a static library is explained at http://www.ritambhara.in/static-vs-dynamic-libraries-in-c/

Dynamic Linking

In dynamic linking, program and library are not combined together at link time. Linker place information in the executable that tells the loader which shared object module has the code and which runtime linker should be used to find and bind the references.

This means that the actual binding between program and the shared object is done at runtime.

Some referenced symbols in the program are not associated with specific code at the link time. Instead, symbols for shared objects are only verified for their validity to ensure that they do exist somewhere and are not yet added into program. Linker stores locations of external libraries to find missing symbols in executable. Effectively, this defers the binding until the runtime.

Programs linked dynamically are linked against the shared objects that usually have extension `.so`. An example of such an object is the shared object version of the standard C library, `libc.so`. Some advantages of dynamic linking are as follows:

- ✓ Size of executable is smaller because they do not have all text and data segments information.
- ✓ It is very useful for portability.
- ✓ Standard libraries can be upgraded without re-linked.
- ✓ Dynamic linking allows two or more processes to share read-only executable modules like standard C libraries and kernel. Since multiple processes are sharing the same libraries, it helps in saving memory.

Question 1. 5: What is Undefined behaviour, Unspecified behaviour and Implementation-defined behaviour?

These terminologies are sometimes used interchangeably by users of C and C++. They are defined in Annex-J of C11 standard.

A program is said to have an **undefined behaviour** when it uses an erroneous construct or erroneous data or any other such thing for which the standard imposes no requirements. The program breaks the rule of language and is not detected until run-time. For example:

- ✓ Dereferencing a dangling pointer.
- ✓ `a/b` or `a%b` when value of b is zero.
- ✓ Using `bsearch` library function on an array that is not sorted.

✓ Array out of bounds.

✓ Behaviour of Integer overflow and underflow.

If the behaviour is undefined, it means that anything can happen either before, after, or while executing the operation. The program may crash, it may delete all files on computer or it may just run fine, anything means just anything can happen. When Code 1.8 is executed:

```
bool* getX(){
   bool x = true;
   return &x;
}

int main()
{
   bool b = *getX();
   if(b)
      printf("\n b IS TRUE");
   if(!b)
      printf("\n b IS NOT TRUE");
}
```

Code 1.8

It is possible that neither of the two messages gets printed, because of dangling pointer. It is also possible that both messages get printed.

We think of bool values as either true or false but not both, but because behaviour is undefined, even that mutual exclusivity is not guaranteed.

Unspecified behaviour is when the standard provides two or more possibilities but does not impose requirements on which should be chosen by a compiler writer. For example, the order in which functions fun1 and fun2 are called in the following expression is not specified:

```
x = fun1() + fun2();
```

Compilers may choose to implement it from left-to-right or right-to-left, resulting in either fun1 or fun2 being called first. Standard does not dictate the order of call. (See *Question 2.3*).

Undefined behaviour results in unpredictable (and erroneous) behaviour of entire program. With unspecified behaviour, program makes a choice at a particular junction and continue as usual, just that we do not know how it makes that choice.

The implementation is not required to document anything about the choices made and can make the choices in a non-deterministic way (may be) depending on compiler options.

There are many unspecified things in C language. Some of them are as follows:

✓ The manner and timing of static initialization.
✓ The termination status returned to the hosted environment if return type of `main` is not compatible with `int`.
✓ The value of padding bytes when storing values in structures or unions.
✓ The order in which subexpressions are evaluated and the order in which side effects take place, except as specified for the function-call `()`, `&&`, `||`, `?:`, and comma operator.
✓ The layout of storage for function parameters on stack frame.
✓ The order in which any side effects occur among the initialization list expressions in an initializer.
✓ The result of rounding when the value is out of range.

Implementation-defined behaviour is similar to unspecified behaviour, except, implementation is required to document results of such operations.

C language standard does not specify results of implementation-defined behaviour, but compiler's documentation must specify the behaviour clearly. Hence, the behaviour has to be deterministic.

These things are part of implementation and not the standard. Some implementation-defined behaviours are as follows:

✓ An alternative manner in which `main` function may be defined. For example, some implementations have a third argument in `main` function giving execution environment, otherwise accessible through `getenv` in `stdlib.h`.

```
int main(int argc, char **argv, char **envp);
```

Some implementations even allow a fourth parameter containing some OS-supplied information, e.g. path to executing binary.
✓ The manner of execution of the string by the `system` function.
✓ Number of bits in a byte.
✓ Which of signed char or unsigned char has the same range, representation, and behaviour as "plain" char.
✓ The results of some bitwise operations on signed integers.

✓ The direction of rounding when a floating-point number is converted to a narrower.

✓ floating-point number.

✓ Result of converting a pointer to an integer and vice-versa.

✓ The size of the result of subtracting two pointers to elements of the same array.

✓ How the named source file is searched for in an included " " delimited header.

✓ The nesting limit for `#include` processing.

✓ The places that are searched for an included < > delimited header, and how the places are specified or the header is identified.

✓ The null pointer constant to which the macro `NULL` expands.

✓ The value of the result of the `sizeof` and `alignof` operators.

In addition to these behaviours, there are also locale-specific behaviour that include things like the format of time and date, direction of writing successive characters and others.

Along with the behaviours, individual implementations may also have some **extensions** that are not portable to other implementations. Like some implementations consider all characters in an identifier name (with or without external linkage) as significant. Other implementations may consider first n characters as significant and ignore characters after that (n varying for implementations).

Some implementations define additional arithmetic types, such as __ `int128` or `double double`, and their appropriate conversions.

The `asm` keyword may be used to insert assembly language directly into the translator output. The most common implementation is via a statement of the form:

```
asm ( character-string-literal );
```

Question 1. 6: What is the maximum value of integer data type in C language?

Amount of memory allocated to a particular data type is implementation-dependent. Compilers are free to choose appropriate sizes for underlining hardware subjected to the following rules:

✓ Size of `int` and `short` is at least 16 bits.

✓ Size of `long` is at least 32 bits.

✓ sizeof(short) ≤ sizeof(int) ≤ sizeof(long). Normally size of `int` is equal to natural word size of machine. With one of either `short` or `long` being equal to `int` in size, but this is not a defined rule.

✓ `long double` is extended-precision floating-point number.

✓ Similar to `short`, `int` and `long`. `float`, `double`, and `long double` can be of same, two different or all different sizes subjected to the following equation.

sizeof(float)≤sizeof(double)≤sizeof(long double)

Header files `limits.h` and `float.h` contain symbolic constants for these sizes. Consider the following entry in file `limits.h`:

```
..............
#define  SHRT_MAX             0x7FFF
#define  SHRT_MIN             ((int)0x8000)
..............
```

The two symbolic constants represent maximum and minimum values of `short` expressed in hexadecimal (`32767` and `-32768`).

Can you write a C language program that prints factorial of a number ? Wait, if you write a program like this:

```
int main()
{
    int n;
    printf("Enter the number :");
    scanf("%d", &n);

    int f=1;
    for(int i=2; i<=n; i++)
        f *= i;

    printf("\nFactorial of %d is %d", n, f);
}
```

When you enter 5, output is:

```
Factorial of 5 is 120
```

Which is equal to 5!. But if you give 100 as input, output may be incorrect. This is because 100! is too big a number to fit into memory allocated to `int` data types. In fact, 100! cannot be accommodated in any primitive data type. The assignment is to write a function that takes an `int` variable as input and print the factorial of that number.

```
void printFactorial(int n);
```

Question 1. 7: What are the different data types?

There are two broad categories of data types in C language.
  1. Primitive data types
  2. User-Defined (or Composite) data types

Primitive data types are the basic, built-in data types that language provides.

Composite data types are defined by developers using guidelines specified by the language, mostly in terms of primitive data types or other composite data types. Figure 1.10 shows the different data types.

size_t (implementation-defined return type of sizeof and alignof), cast to int and enumeration values can also be thought of as a part of integral data types with few exceptions (condition of pre-processor inclusion directive).

Boolean data type was introduced in C99 inside header stdbool.h. Below statement defines an array of two bool elements. bool is defined to be of type _Bool that is large enough to hold 0 and 1.

```
bool arr[2] = {true, false};
```

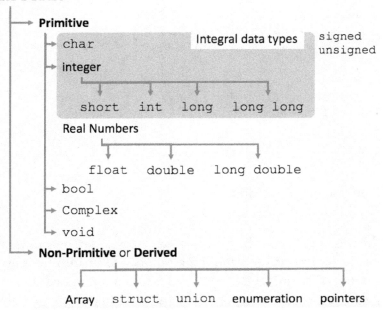

Figure 1.10

In logical expressions, a zero (0, 0.0000, NULL) means logical false and non-zero (2, -4.3, not-null pointers) means logical true. When converting from logical to number, a false become 0 and true become 1.

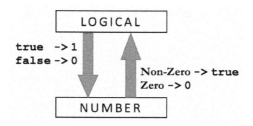

```
int main()
{
  int ivar;
  ivar = 2 > 3;
  printf("%d", ivar);  //0 - because 2>3 is false
  if(-99)
    printf("Hello World"); // -99 is true
}
```

Code 1.9

In Code 1.9, value of ivar printed is zero because expression 2>3 is false, when converted to int is a zero. Hello World is printed because -99 is true (Non-Zero is true).

Question 1. 8: What are literals in C language?

A literal is a constant value. In statement

    x = 2;

x is variable and 2 is a literal. Literals can be of any data type.

Literal type	Example	Description
Character	'a', '@', '2', '\n', '\101'	A character in single quotes or an escape sequence.
String	"A", "Ritambhara", "Big-O ", "#$%@"	Sequence of characters delimited by double quotes. Internally terminated by null character.

Literal type	Example	Description
Integer	2, 3, -123, 043, 0x1a, 0X23F	Octal starts with 0, Hex starts with 0x or 0X. 043 is octal value for 35, 0x1a is hex value for 26.
Unsigned Integer	763U, 3432u, 0543u	Non-negative integers suffixed by u or U.
Long	123L, -543l, 0x1a L, 43758	Integer with suffix l or L or too big to fit into int is taken as long literal.
Unsigned long	123UL, 0x1aul, 43758UL	Integer value with suffix ul or UL.
Float	11.7f, -234.0f, 1.2e+2f	Real value with suffix f or F
Double	11.7, -234.0, 1.2e+2	By default, a real number is double literal
Long double	11.7l, -234.0L, 1.2e+2L	Real value with suffix l or L
Array	{1, 2, 3, 4}	

Character literals are printable (like `'a'`, `'H'`, `'2'`, `'@'`, and so on.) or non-printable characters (like backspace, new-line, tab, form feed) delimited with single quote. A non-printable character can be printed using its ASCII value or by specifying the escape sequence corresponding to that character. For example, the output of the following code:

```
printf("Ritambhara\nTechnologies");
```

Output:
```
Ritambhara
Technologies
```

And the output of the following code:

```
printf("Hello%cWorld", 8); // ASCII for Back-space
```

Output:
```
HellWorld
```

A String literal is a sequence of characters surrounded by double quotes. They are always terminated by a NULL character making the size of a string larger than what it looks (by one character).

NULL is a symbolic constant defined in stdio.h used to mean a zero (not character '0' which has ASCII value 48 but ASCII-0 character). NULL is represented by escape sequence '\0' and has integer value 0.

Understanding of literals comes handy in some questions like the following:

Question 1. 9: What is the output of the following code?

```
float x = 4.2;
if(x == 4.2)
   printf("HELLO");
else
   printf("BYE");
```

Code 1.10

You may be expecting the output to be HELLO, but the output is BYE. double data type is double precession floating point and float is a single precession format. It literally means that memory allocated to double variables is twice the memory allocated to float variables. i.e if float variables are allocated 4 bytes of memory then double variables are stored in 8 bytes of memory.

For simplicity let us assume 1 byte for float and 2 bytes for double values. Further let us assume that half of the total bits are used to store the mantissa and the other half (grey area below) is used to store exponent.

4.2 literal is of type double, and its binary representation is

00000100.00110011.

The fractional part (.2) when converted to binary number systems is a non-terminating number, but because the memory bits are limited, only 8 bits of this fractional part are stored in the memory. Now when this number is stored in a float variable x, then some of the fractional value will be lost.

0100.0011

We are comparing x and 4.2 in the statement:

```
if(x == 4.2)
```

when float and double values are compared, then float value is promoted to double type, so

```
0100.0011
```

When promoted to double becomes

```
00000100.00110000
```

So, effectively we are comparing the following values:

```
if(00000100.00110000 == 00000100.00110011)
```

The two are not equal, hence the else part is executed and output is BYE. What will be the output, if the code is changed as follows:

```
float x = 4.5;
if(x == 4.5)
  printf("HELLO");
else
  printf("BYE");
```

The double and float values in binary representation of 4.5 are

```
00000100.10000000          0100.1000
```
Double   **Float**

When float value 0100.1000 is promoted to double, it becomes, 00000100.10000000 which is exactly same as the binary representation of double 4.5. In this case, the output is HELLO because there is no loss in converting from double to float.

A way to fix the issue in Code 1.10 is to stop the promotion and compare two single precession values:

```
if(x == 4.2f)
```

4.2f is a single precession floating point literal. Because of this (non-intutive) loss of precession, it is not recommended to use strict equality while comparing floating-point values.

Question 1. 10: What are storage classes in C?

Storage classes define the area of allocated memory, scope of use and life-time of variables and functions defined in a C language program.

There are four storage classes automatic, register, global and static. Out of these automatic and register applies to only data whereas global and static can be used with functions as well. Global storage class provides external linkage and static provides internal linkage. We will take them one by one and then summarize the results.

Automatic

✓ This is the default storage class for non-static local variables defined inside a block (between { and }). There is no need to explicitly use keyword `auto` in the declaration.

✓ Their scope is local to the block in which they are defined. However, within the same function they can be accessed outside the block using pointers.

```
int main()
{
  int a = 5;   // same as, "auto int a = 5;"
  int *ptr;
  {
    int b = 10;   // same as "auto int b = 10;"
    ptr = &b;
  }
  printf("%d", *ptr); // OK. Print 10.
  Printf("%d", b);    // ERROR. Can't access b
}
```

b can only be accessed inside the block in which it is defined.

✓ A local variable can be explicitly specified automatic by placing keyword `auto` in declaration (but it is not required).
`auto int x;`
If `auto` is not available as a keyword in C, life would have been unchanged because it is the default data type. Storage modifier can be placed in any order with respect to the data type and qualifier.

✓ When not explicitly initialized, the default value of `auto` variables is garbage (not-defined).

✓ `auto` variables are allocated memory in activation record of the function in which they are declared.

✓ Formal parameters of function are also auto.

Register

✓ Automatic variables, when declared `register` is a request to compiler to store them in CPU register rather than memory. However since number and size of registers are limited, not every `register` variable may actually get stored inside register, thus it is up to compiler to allocate space to register variables in memory when needed.

✓ Automatic variables and formal parameters can be declared `register` as follows:

```
register int x;
```

storage modifier can be placed in any order with respect to the data type and qualifier.

✓ Register variables cannot be referenced. i.e You cannot apply address-of *&* operator on them.

✓ Since register variables are automatic variables, their default value is garbage.

✓ Compiler may perform optimization and keep copy of frequently used variables in register even if they are not declared `register`. In this case the variable will behave like normal variable of its own storage class. Usually loop iterators are kept in register till the loop is executing and later their original copy in memory is updated with the new value.

Global

✓ Global is not a keyword. Variables declared outside all the functions (and are not static) are global variables. Functions are also global unless explicitly specified as static (*Global variables have same kind of linkage as that of functions*).

✓ Global variables are allocated memory in data area at load-time.

✓ Default value of global variables is zero. All global variables are initialized (to the value given or zero) at load-time, before `main` function is called.

✓ They remain accessible to every function in all files in the entire program (wherever the file in which they are defined is accessible). And if one function changes their value, it is reflected everywhere else (because all of them are accessing the same copy).

✓ Lifetime of a global variable is equal to that of the program. They are allocated memory at load-time, before `main` function is called and the memory gets free after the `main` function returns.

Static

✓ An object is declared static using keyword `static` in its declaration.
`static int ivar;`

✓ Like global variables, static variables are also load-time variables. Memory to these variables are allocated before the `main` function is called and remains thru the lifetime of the program.

✓ Static variables are also allocated memory in the data area.

✓ If not explicitly initialized, static variables are initialized to zero by default. This initialization is done at load-time, before `main` function is called.

✓ Static comes in two flavors.

• If a local variable of a function is declared `static`, then its scope is local, i.e can only be accessed inside the block, but its storage is in data-area outside function's activation record.

It will hence retain its value in successive function calls (unlike automatic variables that are allocated memory on stack and the memory is freed when function returns).

• If an external variable (declared outside all functions) or function is declared `static` then it only change the scope of that variable (or function).

```
static int x; // external variable

static void fun();   // static function

int main(){...} // Main function
```

Variable x is allocated memory in data-area and its life-time is equal to the program. The x and function `fun` will both have internal linkage. Both of them can only be accessed within the same file where they are defined. They cannot be accessed in any other file (even when they are global).

This comes handy if you are using two variables or functions by the same name in different files which are compiled together. Declare both of them as `static`.

Understanding of storage class helps us in answering many questions as following:

Question 1. 11: Why does the following code prints the values mentioned in the comments for variables ivar?

```
int ivar = 20;
int main()
{
  int ivar = 10;
  {
    int ivar = 5;
    printf("%d", ivar); // PRINT 5
  }
  printf("%d", ivar);        // PRINT 10
}
void dummyfunc(){
  printf("%d", ivar);        // PRINT 20 - Global ivar
}
```

We cannot define two variables with same name in same scope. But we can define them in nested scopes. And within a particular scope local variable gets preference over global variable.

In `main`, ivar=10 overwrite global definition ivar=20 and in inner (nested) block ivar=5 overwrite ivar=10; but being an automatic variable its scope is restricted till end of block after which ivar=10 is the most local copy of `ivar` available. In function `dummyfunc`, only one global definition of `ivar` is available.

Question 1. 12: What is the output of the following code?

```
int igvar;
int main()
{
  fun();
```

```
    fun();
    fun();
}
void fun()
{
    int iauto = 5;
    static int istat;
    iauto = iauto + 10;
    istat = istat + 10;
    printf("\nAuto: %d, Static: %d", iauto, istat);
}
```

Output of preceding code is:
```
Auto: 15, Static: 10
Auto: 15, Static: 20
Auto: 15, Static: 30
```

Because `auto` variables are initialized every time function is called while `static` variables are initialized only once (at load-time) and they retain their (updated) value in the successive function calls (because they reside in data-area outside activation record of function).

We have not initialized variable `istat` in the previous example, being a load-time variable, it was initialized by zero. What if we initialize it with a local variable.

```
int iauto = 5;
static int istat = iauto; // ERROR
```

This is Error, because

Load-time variables can only be initialized with constants.

If the picture of memory is clear in our mind, we can answer such questions using common sense. Have a look at time-line shown in Question 1.3:

1. When program is loading, variable `istat` is allocated memory (in data-area) and initialized.
2. After loading is complete, `main` function is called.
3. The `main` function in turn calls function `fun`.
4. When function `fun` is called, its activation record is created on the stack and in that activation record memory to `iauto` is allocated. And then `iauto` is initialized with 5.

We are trying to initialize `istat` variable in step-1, with a value of `iauto` that will be available in step-4. Hence, error.

Similarly, following initialization is also error:

```
static int x = strlen("Hello");
```

`strlen` is a function in `string.h` header. This function can only be called when the loading is complete. And one of the tasks in the loading process is to allocate memory to static variables and initialize them. Hence, error. However, the following statements are fine:

```
int main()
{
   static int x;
   x = strlen("Hello");
}
```

Here `x` is initialized to zero during load-time and while executing `main`, `strlen` function is called and its return value is assigned to `x` (initialization v/s assignment).

Question 1. 13: Which of the following programs will take less time to execute and why?

```
int main(){                    int main(){
   int ivar= 0;                   register int ivar=0;
   for(ivar = 0;                  for(ivar = 0;
       ivar<1000;                     ivar<1000;
       ivar++)                        ivar++)
       ;                              ;
}                              }
```

The only difference between the two is the use of keyword `register`. In first program `ivar` is an automatic integer variable while in second it is `register` integer variable. Ideally, second program should execute faster than first one, but on my system both programs are taking the exact same time. Why?

Compiler may perform certain optimizations on our code to make it execute faster. One of the optimizations is to keep a copy of an automatic variable in register without accessing it from memory every time it is accessed (even if it is not declared `register`). So `ivar` in the first program is kept inside register without accessing a fresh new copy from memory every time, making the two programs exactly same.

If you do not want compiler to perform this optimization on a variable, then you can declare that variable as `volatile`. It is a qualifier that does the opposite of register and force the compiler to get a fresh copy of variable from memory each time we access it.

Question 1. 14: What is prototyping and what are extern variables ?

If the function declaration is not visible at the point of function-call, then compiler (prior to C99) assumes the function to be of default type. C99 has made it compulsory to have explicit function declarations in such cases. Consider the following code, it will give compile-time error:

Example:
```
#define PI 3.14
int main(){
    int radius = 2;
    printf("Area = %lf", area(radius));
}
double area(int r){
    return PI * r * r;
}
```

You have to inform the compiler about the function before the function call is made. In above code, function definition comes later, and at the point of call, compiler does not have any information about the function to make a decision whether or not this call is correct.

Prototype of a functions gives all information about the function without defining the function. The following code will not give any error:

```
#define PI 3.14
double area(int r); //Prototype of function.
int main(){
    int radius = 2;
    printf("Area = %lf", area(radius));
}
```

```
double area(int r){ // Actual function.
  return PI * r * r;
}
```

Another way, off course is to physically put the definition of function area above main.

If only prototype of function is given, and actual definition does not exist, then compiler will not complain, but in the link phase, when linker looks for actual function definition, it will fail.

If a function is defined in one and used in another compilation unit, then the definition of function will be resolved at link-time.

Similar to function prototyping, every variable must be declared before it is used and declaration must be visible at compile-time. Definition serves as declaration. The following code will give compile-time error:

```
int main(){
  printf("%d", x); //COMPILE-TIME ERROR
}
int x = 4;
```

The definition of x is not visible at the point of its use. extern declaration act as a prototype declaration for variables. The following code will work fine:

```
//DECLARATION OF x (NO MEM ALLOCATED)
extern int x;
int main(){
  printf("%d", x); //OK
}
int x = 4;   // DEFINITION.
```

No memory is allocated for extern declarations. They are just an indication to the compiler, that definition will be found during the link phase. If we have just the declaration and not the definition:

```
extern int x; //DECLARATION OF x
int main(){
  printf("%d", x); //ERROR AT LINK TIME
}
```

The compiler will not complain because, `extern` declaration assures the compiler that definition will be available during the link phase. Compiler, believes this and put the stub for the linker to find the actual definition. Linker will complain because it could not find the definition. The statement

```
extern int x;
```

is only declaration and does not allocate any memory space to variable `x`. And below statement is definition

```
int x = 4;
```

We can have multiple `extern` declarations (like multiple function prototype), but there should be only one definition in one scope. We cannot initialize `extern` declaration, because no physical memory is allocated against those declarations. If initial value is given, then it will be considered as definition. Following is a compile-time error (it is also acting as definition of `x`, hence multiple definitions).

```
extern int x = 10;
```

Though not used much, `extern` keyword can also be used in function declaration.

```
extern double area(int r);          /* NO ERROR */
```

Global variables and functions have same kind of internal and external linkage. Both can be made static to restrict their usage to the same file (internal linkage) and both can be used in other files as well, the two files being linked at link-time (external linkage).

Question 1. 15: What are Type Qualifiers ?

A type qualifier is applied to a data type to add some additional value to the type. Following are the type qualifiers

volatile

When a variable is declared `volatile`, no implementation specific optimizations are performed on that variable. In *Question 1.13* we saw that compiler may treat variable `ivar` in the following code as `register`:

```
int main()
{
   int ivar = 0;
   for(ivar = 0; ivar<1000; ivar++)
       ;
}
```

Compiler choose to update the copy in register, and later (after the execution of loop) this value is copied back to the memory.

If ivar can be changed from outside this code, and if its value become 2000 when the value in register copy is just 100, then compiler will not even acknowledge this change until the loop ends.

The problem is because of local optimization performed on variable ivar. When a variable is declared volatile, no optimization is performed on that variable. Whenever its value is desired, a fresh copy is fetched from the RAM always, and when the value change, it is written back to RAM.

Const

When a const keyword is applied in the definition it announces that value of variable cannot be changed.

It is discussed in detail in *Question 7.5*.

Restrict

C99 introduce restrict keyword. When it is used with a pointer, it indicates, that in the lifetime of this pointer it is the only one thru which that memory is accessed. This allows compiler to generate more optimized code.

Question 1. 16: What are the signatures of printf and scanf functions?

printf and scanf functions are declared in header stdio.h. They are among the most used functions in the library, esp. if you are writing small programs in an interview. scanf is used to read formatted data from the keyboard (default input device) and printf is used to write formatted data to the screen (default output device). Inside stdio.h, these functions are declared as:

```
int scanf(const char *format, ...);
int printf(const char *format, ...);
```

scanf scans the format string and read characters according to specifications in the format string and store results at locations specified by remaining arguments following format. All arguments after format are pointers (*A pointer is an address in the memory. An ampersand is a pointer operator that returns address of its operand.* &ch *means address of* ch). The following statement

```
scanf("%d%c", &intNumber, &ch);
```

expects you to enter one integer and one character separated by one or more white spaces (blank space, tab, new line, carriage return, vertical tab, or form feed character or a sequence of these). If format specifier %d is used, the value entered is received as an integer. Similarly, there are format specifiers for other data types as well.

After processing entire format string character-by-character, scanf returns number of values it is able to read successfully. The following statement outputs 2.

```
printf("Number of values read: %d",
       scanf("%d%c", &intNumber, &ch));
```

Output:

```
Number of values read: 2
```

printf complements scanf by printing to standard output according to the specifications in format string. It keeps on printing format to output stream till it gets a conversion specification which when encountered results in printing of next argument in succession. Following is the list of conversion characters:

character	Argument type	character	Argument type
%c	Single character	%s	String
%d, %i	Integer	%u	Unsigned Integer
%f, %e	float	%x	Unsigned hex
%o	Unsigned octal	%%	Prints % char
%lf	double	%ll	long long

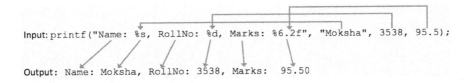

Input: `printf("Name: %s, RollNo: %d, Marks: %6.2f", "Moksha", 3538, 95.5);`

Output: Name: Moksha, RollNo: 3538, Marks: 95.50

`printf` returns the number of characters printed. The output of the following code is `Hello5`

```
printf("%d", printf("Hello"));
```

The inner `printf` prints `Hello` and return `5` (number of characters printed), and outer `printf` prints the value returned by the inner `printf`.

Imagine if an interviewer asks you to find the length of a string without using any string function like `strlen` and without using any loop (*Good interviewers don't ask such trick questions. But, not every interviewer is good*).

```
char str[] = "Ritambhara Technologies";
int length = printf("%s", str);
```

`printf` prints the string and return number of characters printed, i.e the length of string.

Question 1. 17: What is the difference between `typedef` and `#define` ?

Following points discuss the differences between `typedef` and `#define`

Pre-processor versus Compiler

`#define` is handled by the pre-processor that replace the values from point of definition to the point of use. `typedef` is handled by the compiler and is an actual definition of a new type. All `#define` are resolved before its control reach the compiler and `typedef` are considered. There are some implications of this fact:

✓ `typedef` is a statement and must be terminated with semicolon, `#define` is a directive and should not be terminated with semicolon.

✓ There can be side effects of replacement in `#define`, For example:

```
typedef char* string_t;
```

```
#define string_d char*

string_t s1, s2; // Both s1 and s2 are char*
string_d s3, s4; // s3 is char* s4 is a char
```

The pre-processor replace second declaration as:

```
char* s3, s4;
```

Which means that `s3` is of type `char*` but `s4` is of type `char` (`*` has to be specified with all variables if we want all of them to be pointers, like `char *s3, *s4;`).

✓ `typedef` follows scope rule i.e if a new type is defined in a scope (inside a function), the new type name is visible only in that scope. Pre-processor does not know scope. It replaces all occurrences found after `#define`. For example:

```
int main()
{
  { // NEW SCOPE
    typedef int myInt_t;
    #define myInt_d int

    myInt_t a;        // OK.
    myInt_d b;        // OK.
  }

  myInt_t c;      // ERROR. myInt_t not found
  myInt_d d;      // OK.
}
```

Macro v/s type alias

`#define` is used to define macros also, but `typedef` can only be used to provide a new name for already existing type (it cannot create a new type). Similarly, `#define` is also used to define compile-time constants like the following:

```
#define N 10
```

It can be used for named-constants. `typedef` cannot be used for any other purpose but giving new name for already defined types.

`typedef` **as type alias**

There are certain type definitions which you can only define using `ty-pedef` and not `#define`. Consider the following cases:

1. New name can be given to an integer array of size 10, as:

```
typedef int arr[10];
```

2. When there are more than one words in the type name (like `unsigned int`).

```
typedef unsigned int UINT;
```

We cannot define such a type using `#define`.

3. For giving new name to struct types, like:

```
typedef struct
{
    int x;
    int y;
}POINT;
```

Question 1. 18: What are identifiers and why we cannot have an identifier name starting with numeric digit?

Apart from keywords, literals and programming syntax, everything in a C program is treated as Identifier. The function names, variables names, user-defined type name, name given to constants are all identifiers.

An identifier can consist of alphabets (upper case, lower case), digits (0-9) and _ (underscore) character. But it must not start with a number.

Valid Identifier Names	Invalid Identifier names
num_1	1num
_num1	1_num
Num_	365_days
iNt	int
Char	char
Continue	continue
CONTINUE	23

We know that `math.h` header defined constant macro `M_PI`. It is fine to have a variable with this name in our program if we do not include `math.h`.

```
#include <stdio.h>
```

```
int main(){
  int M_PI = 3.14;
  ... ...
}
```

If we include `math.h`, then this code will not compile because `M_PI` will be replaced with the `double` value.

We cannot have two identifiers with the same name in the same scope. The identifiers we define should not conflict with the identifiers defined in the headers included in our program. Probably this is the reason why identifiers defined in library header files start with underscore. Remember the following with regards to naming variables and functions:

✓ Do not create unnecessarily long variable names. The compiler may ignore characters in the name after a certain length. At least 63 initial characters of internal name (local internal to a function) and 31 characters of external name (function name, global variables and global type names) are significant. Exact size is implementation dependent.

Similarly, there is a limit on number of identifiers allowed in a block and translation unit. Avoid using underscore as first character in the name because many library variables start with underscore.

✓ Identifier names are case-sensitive. `sum`, `Sum`, `SUM` are different. We can have a variable name `Int` that does not conflict with the reserve word `int`. But avoid using such names.

Let us now ponder over, why cannot we name a variable starting with a number. There is no officially defined reason for this, but it may be because of following reasons (besides being confusing):

As discussed in *Question 1.2*, the Lexical analyser (during compilation) read the program and generate tokens. It usually read the program character-by-character.

The value of a number starting with a digit can be computer by traversing the digits forward, without a need to read the number again. For example, if token is 25, when the first digit is found to be 2, we know it has to be a number, so 2 is stored as a value, when 5 is found, the previous value is multiplied with 10 and 5 is added to it, giving 25.

If first character of identifiers can also be numeric, then parser cannot decide after reading 2 whether the token is numeric literal or identifier. So it may not be possible to generate tokens in linear time by reading the program in just forward sequence because the parser may have to move back and forth.

If identifier names are allowed to start with numbers, then an extra restriction need to be added that identifiers must have an alphabet following the digit(s). Otherwise variable name "10" would be indistinguishable from the literal 10. This would have affected the performance of parser.

Another challenge is that C language use alphabet suffix to fix type of numeric values. For example, `25u` is a valid numeric literal.

2.

OPERATORS AND STATEMENTS

Question 2. 1: Give the list of all operators available in C?

C is very rich in operators. There are arithmetic operators, relational, logical, bitwise, pointer operators, structure operators and so on. even assignment and comma are operators in C. The only exception is unavailability of an exponential operator.

Table 2.1 list all operators with their associativity in order of their precedence, the ones listed above have higher precedence and operators in the same row have same precedence.

Row No.	Associativity	Operators
1.	Left to Right	()　　[]　　->　　.　　++ (post)　　-- (post)
2.	Right to Left	!　　~　　++ (pre)　　-- (pre)　　+　　-　　(type)　　* (value-at)　　& (Address-of)　sizeof
3.	Left to Right	*　　/　　%
4.	Left to Right	+　-
5.	Left to Right	<<　　>>
6.	Left to Right	<　　<=　　>　　>=
7.	Left to Right	==　　!=
8.	Left to Right	&
9.	Left to Right	^
10.	Left to Right	|
11.	Left to Right	&&
12.	Left to Right	||
13.	Right to Left	? :
14.	Right to Left	=　　+=　　-=　　*=　　/=　　%=　　&=　　^=　　|=　<<=　　>>=
15.	Left to Right	,

Table 2.1

Next, we discuss these operator row-by-row.

Row No. 1: Function call operator, () calls function on its left side and pass all comma separated list within parenthesis as arguments to it. Subscript operator, [] is used with arrays to access element at a particular index in an array, structure arrow -> and structure dot operator. are used to access members of a structure.

All of these operators are covered in detail in later chapters. An important thing to understand here is that associativity of these operators is left to right. i.e. when more than one operators from this row are used in an expression, they are applied from left to right.

head->next->data first compute head->next and then (head->next)->data.

Row No. 2: This row has unary operators with associativity right to left. Right-to-Left associativity means, if two operators (with equal precedence) are applied in an expression, the one on the right side will be applied first, followed by one on the left side. Let us understand each operator in this row.

! is logical NOT operator. It toggles logical value of its operand. If operand is non-zero (true), result is 0 (false) and if operand is zero (false), result is 1 (true).

```
x = !5;        // x will be 0.
x = !-20;      // x will be 0.
x = !0;        // x will be 1.
x = !!234;     // x will be 1 (!234=0 and !0=1)
x = !(2>4);    // x will be 1 (2>4 is 0 and !0=1)
x = !2>4;      // x will be 0 (Evaluated as (!2)>4)
```

In last example, precedence of ! operator is higher than > operator, which intern is higher than =. Expression is evaluated as follows:

```
(x = ((!2) > 4));
```

where !2 is 0 and 0>4; is false i.e. 0. In fact expression !y>4 will always be false irrespective of the value of y.

The output of logical NOT operator is always either 0 or 1.

~ is a unary bitwise NOT operator. All bitwise operators are only applied on integral operands. Bitwise NOT returns one's complement of its operand.

Bitwise-NOT (~) and logical-NOT (!) operators are discussed in detail in *Question 6.2*.

++ and −− are increment and decrement operators respectively. They can only be applied to integral and pointer variables. Operand of these operators must have an associated 1-value (cannot be a literal).

Increment operator adds 1 and decrement operator subtracts 1 from operand.

Both of them can be applied as prefix or postfix. ++n is pre-incrementing n and n++ is post incrementing n. Both pre and post increment increase the value of n by 1, the difference is that ++n increase the value of n before it is used where as n++ increment n after its value is used. Similarly −−n and n−− both decrement n but uses the decremented and non-decremented value of n respectively. In following code

```
int x = 9;
int y = ++x;
```

value of y is 10, if we change it to post-increment

```
int x = 9;
int y = x++;
```

then value of y will be 9. In both the cases, x is incremented to 10.

Precedence of post-increment/decrement is higher than that of pre-increment/decrement. Associativity of post-increment/decrement is left to right and associativity of pre-increment/decrement is right to left. In C++, ++i can be used as l-value, but i++ cannot be, but, in C language none of them can be used as l-value.

Following expressions are errors:

Expression	Error Description
2++;	Lvalue required error. Cannot apply to literals.
−−3;	Lvalue required error. Cannot apply to literals.
(x+y)++	Lvalue required error. x+y has only rvalue.
(x++)++	Lvalue required error. Result of increment and decrement is a literal and does not have an lValue.

These operators come handy in many situations, they make code more readable and compact. Consider the push and pop operations in a stack data structure.

```
void push(int data)                int pop()
{                                  {
  if(top < N-1)                      if(top == -1)
    S[++top] = data;                   printf("Underflow");
  else                               else
    printf("Overflow");                return S[top--];
}                                  }
```

If top = 3, statement
```
return S[top--];
```

Returns S[3] and decrement top to 2. It is equivalent to the following statements.
```
int temp = S[top];
top = top - 1;
return temp;
```

+ and − in this row are unary plus and unary minus operator. Unary plus + is a dummy operator and usually no executable code is generated for it. Unary minus toggle sign of its operand.

Unary, *(value-at) and &(address-of) are pointer operators. They are discussed in detail in *Chapter-3*.

sizeof is the only operator applied at compile time. It returns an unsigned int (defined in <stddef.h> as size_t) value, equal to the memory allocated in bytes to its operand. Operand can be a data type or an expression as shown in the following code:

```
sizeof(type)
sizeof(expression)
```

type is either a predefined data type (int, float, double etc.) or user defined data type (struct, union, enum, and so on.).

```
printf("%d %d %d", sizeof(int), sizeof(2+4.5)
                 , sizeof("a"));
```

Output: 4 8 2

What gets printed is the number of bytes allocated to `int`, `double` and an array of two `char`. The output may be different for different systems. Please note, compiler change this `printf` to the following:

```
printf("%d %d %d", 4, 8, 2);
```

If executable generated with above `printf` is then taken to a machine with different architecture, where size of these data types is different, the program may not work as expected.

(type) is cast operator used for explicit type-casting. It converts the operand on right side to type `type`. If operand is not convertible to `type`, a compile-time error is generated.

Some conversions happen implicitly, without any need for explicit type-casting, like following promotion from `int` to `double`:

```
double x = 3;
```

In this conversion, we are not losing any value. The reverse, however, is a lossy conversion:

```
int x = 3.75;
```

value of `x` is 3 and `.75` is lost. Most compilers flash a warning on this statement about the possible loss of value. If an explicit cast is used, there won't be any warning.

```
int x = (int)3.75;
```

The most rampant example of explicit casting is return type of `malloc` function. `malloc` allocates memory in heap and return address of allocated memory as a `void` pointer, this needs to be explicitly casted to specific type, otherwise the code will not compile.

```
int* iptr = (int*) malloc(sizeof(int));
```

Row No. 3 & 4: Row 3 and 4 has binary arithmetic operators multiplication(*), division(/), modulo(%), addition(+), and subtract(-).

If arguments of division operator are both integers, result is also integer. Value of expression

```
5/9*9
```

is zero (and not 5). Because of left-to-right associativity, division is performed before multiplication. Result of `5/9` is 0 because fractional part is truncated (both 5 and 9 are `int` so result is also `int`). Hence the answer is also zero. However, `9*5/9` is 5 because multiplication is performed before division.

Modulo operator returns remainder and can only be applied on integral operands. `a%b` is equal to remainder when `a` is divided by `b`. Expression `4.5%2` is a compile-time error.

The result of both `/` and `%` is undefined if second operand is zero.

Row No. 5: Row 5 has binary bitwise operators, bitwise left shift `<<` and bitwise right shift `>>`. Like other bitwise operators they can only be applied to integral operands. Expression

```
ivar << n
```

shifts binary representation of `ivar` left by `n` bits, filling `n` empty spaces at right with zero-bits. Effect of single left shift is same as multiplication by 2 (See *Question 6.12*). Similarly, effect of right-shift is division-by-two.

If any of the two arguments is negative, the result is unspecified. Results of `1<<-1`, `-1<<1` and `-1<<-1` is not clearly defined. The result is also undefined when second argument is more than number of bits in the binary representation of argument on left side.

As a thumb rule, apply bit-wise operations on unsigned integrals only.

After executing the following statements:`int x = 3;`

```
int y = x << 2;
```

`x` is unchanged and `y` becomes 12 (`0...00011<<2 = 0...01100`). Its analogous to `y=x+2;` Result of shift operator is an rvalue.

Row No. 6 & 7: Row-6 has less-than(`<`), greater-than(`>`), less-than-or-equal-to(`<=`), and greater-than-or-equal-to(`>=`). Row-7 has equality operators; equal-to(`==`)and not-equal-to(`!=`).

Result of all these operators is logical, either `0`(`false`) or `1`(`true`). Equality operators are not recommended for floating-point numbers, having non-zero fractional part, because of possibility of non-terminating binary fractional part as shown in *Question 1.9*. Following code:

```
float f = 0;
```

```
for(f = 0.1; f != 1.0; f = f + 0.1)
  printf("Love");
```

prints Love infinitely (not 9 times) and you will agree that this much of Love is lethal to your program.

Decimal 0.1 when converted to binary is a non-terminating number. Because of this, actual value stored in f is not exactly 0.1 but an approximation. During the iterations, value of f is never exactly equal to 1.0 (it will be about 0.999999 and then 1.00001) and the loop never terminates.

A simple change in the condition can make the code work:

```
float f = 0;
for(f = 0.1; f < 1.0; f = f + 0.1)
  printf("Love");
```

Row No. 8, 9 & 10: These rows have bitwise operators. All bitwise operators can only be applied on integral operands.

We are revising this thrice in the same section – Good!.

Row-8 has bitwise AND(&), Row-9 has bitwise Exclusive-OR(^), and Row-10 has bitwise OR(|). Let's summarize all bitwise operators:

```
~           Bitwise NOT
<<  >>      Left Shift / Right Shift
&           Bitwise AND
^           Bitwise X-OR
|           Bitwose OR
```

Following truth table shows these operations on a single bit:

A	B	!A	A&B	A|B	A^B
0	0	1	0	0	0
0	1	1	0	1	1
1	0	0	0	1	1
1	1	0	1	1	0

Chapter-6 is dedicated to bit-wise operators and bit twiddling.

Row No. 11 & 12: Row 11 and 12 has logical AND(&&), and logical OR(||), operators respectively.

Result of all logical operations is either true(1) or false(0). Result of && is 1 if both operands are non-zero. Result of || is 1 if either of the two operand is non-zero.

The order of evolution of operands for these operators is strictly defined from left to right (See *Question 2.3*). Left operand is evaluated first and right operator is evaluated only if left operand is unable to establish the truth or falsehood of entire expression.

Consider the following piece of code:

```
x = 5;
y = 2>3 && x++ == 6;
printf("%d : %d", x, y);
```

Output: 5 : 0

y is false because expression on right side is false. Left operand of && is evaluated first. 2>3 is false, it means final value of the entire expression will be false, irrespective of value of sub-expression on right side of &&. Sub-expression on right side, x++ == 6 is therefore never evaluated and value of x remains unchanged. Similarly, following statement does not change the value of x.

```
y = 2<3 || x++ == 6;
```

This is called **short-circuit evaluation**. The code should be written in a way that such side-effects does not occur.

Good programmers use this short-circuit evaluation intelligently. Following statement results in a run-time error if value of den is zero:

```
if(num/den == 10){
  printf("num is 10 times of den");
}
```

a small check can make it run for all values of den

```
if(den != 0 && num/den == 10){
  printf("num is 10 times of den");
}
```

Expression num/den == 10 is evaluated only if den is non-zero.

Row No. 13: Conditional operator (?:) take three arguments and is the only ternary operator. It provides an alternate and easy way to write simple if-else conditions. Following three codes are exactly same:

1.
```if(x>0)```
   ```modx=x;```
```else```
   ```modx=-x;```
	2.
	   ```modx = (x>0) ? x : -x;```
	
	3.
	   ```(x>0) ? (modx= x) : (modx= -x);```

Syntax of conditional operator is:

```
expr1 ? expr2 : expr3
```

`expr1` is evaluated for its logical value. If it is `true`, `expr2` is evaluated else `expr3` is evaluated. Result of entire expression is either `expr2` or `expr3` whichever is evaluated.

In Code-2, it is not compulsory to put a parenthesis around `x>0` because conditional operator has lower precedence than `>` operator. But in Code-3 a parenthesis around `modx = -x` is required because of lower precedence of assignment operator `=`. Following expression results in a compile-time error:

```
(x>0) ? (modx= x) : modx= -x;
```

Because it gets evaluated as

```
((x>0) ? (modx= x) : modx)= -x
```

and left side of assignment is not lvalue (See *Question 3.1*).

Row No. 14: Operators in this row are assignment and compound assignment operators. They require operand on left to be an lvalue (See *Question 3.1*) where result of right-side expression can be stored.

```
expr1 = expr2
```

is an assignment expression and

```
expr1 = expr2;
```

is assignment statement. In both cases, `expr2` is evaluated and its value is stored at lvalue associated with `expr1`. Type of assignment expression is the type of `expr1` and value of assignment expression is value assigned to `expr1`. Value of expression

```
a = 9
```

is 9. It is this value that makes following expression possible.

```
b = a = 9
```

because it is evaluated as b=(a=9).

Compound assignment operator is of the form op= where op is any of the following binary operators:

```
+  -  *  /  %  &  ^  |  <<  >>
```

It is actually an easy way of writing an assignment expression. Expression

```
x = x + 1
```

can also be written as

```
x += 1
```

differences between assignment expression

```
exp1 = exp1 op exp2
```

and corresponding operator assignment expression

```
exp1 op = exp2
```

is the following:

In assignment operator exp1 is evaluated twice (once for left side and once for right side of assignment operator) but in compound assignment operator it is evaluated only once. If there are any side effects to exp1 then the two expressions may be different.

Expression exp1 op= exp2 is actually equivalent to exp1 = (exp1) op (exp2) (except for above fact). If value of a is 2 then

```
a *= 2+3;
```

will set a to 10 which is same as

```
a = a * (2+3);
```

and not

```
a =  a * 2 + 3; .
```

Compound assignment operator helps compiler produce efficient code. Note that ! = is not a compound assignment operator but logical not-equal-to operator.

Row No. 15: Comma is a unique operator in C. One because the order of evolution of comma operator is defined from left to right. The result and type of the total expression is same as that of right operand. Left operand is evaluated as side effect. In the following expression:

```
int x = 3; int y = 5;
a = (x++, ++y);
```

value of a is 6. x++ is evaluated as a side effect and will change the value of x to 4.

But comma is not always an operator, it also acts as "a separator", and when it acts as a separator, the order of evolution is not defined.

Comma acts as a separator when used in function calls to separate the arguments. For example, the output of following printf is not defined

```
printf("%d%d", ++x,++x);
```

because the order in which the three arguments of printf function gets evaluated is unspecified.

Comma operator can be used to write compact code, you can actually write more than one statements sequentially without any alteration in the meaning. For example, the following do-while loop

```
count = 0;
do{
   count++;
   ch = getch();
}while(ch != EOF);
```

calculates the number of characters entered till user enters an EOF character. It can be written using a comma operator as follows:

```
count = 0;
while(count++, ch=getch(), ch!=EOF);
```

The final condition is ch!=EOF, the other two expressions are evaluated as side effects. For that matter any do-while loop

```
do{
   stm1;
   stm2;
   ... ...
   stmN;
}while(con);
```

can be written as while loop

```
while(stm1, stm2, ......, stmN, con);
```

This while loop evaluates stm1, then stm2, and so on till stmN and finally con. If con is non-zero, loop is executed again else control move out of loop which is exactly same as the do-while loop. But, obviously writing such obfuscated code should be discouraged because it is not that readable.

Question 2. 2: How will the below array change after following operations?

```
int a[] = {1,2,3,4};
int i = 2;
a[i] = i++;
```

Answer is unspecified. When a variable is used in an expression and is also updated in the same expression, the value of the variable being used is not defined.

What do you think should be the output of printf in the below code?

```
int a = 4;
printf("%d %d", a++, a++);
```

Answer is again unspecified, because order of evolution of function arguments is not specified. Note that comma is not an operator here, it is a separator used to separate the function arguments.

Increment and decrement operators should be cautiously used because at times they may result in side effects. For example, if fun() is a function which accept two integers and it is called as follows:

```
fun(x, x++);
```

then values passed to fun is unspecified. Call to fun1 in *Code 2.1* is slightly different

```
void fun1(int);
main(){
   fun1( (2,3) );
}
void fun1(int a){
   printf("%d", a);
}
```

Code 2.1

(2,3) is a single expression whose output is 3. Note inner parenthesis in function call `fun1((2,3))` is actually only one value because comma is an operator here, thanks to the parenthesis.

Question 2. 3: What is the output of Code 2.2?

```
int x;

int fun1(){
   x = 5;
   return 2;
}

int fun2(){
   x = 10;
   return 3;
}

int main()
{
   int sum = fun1() + fun2();
   printf("%d", x);
   return 0;
}
```

Code 2.2

Initially x is 0. `fun1` change x to 5 and return (hard-coded) 2. `fun2` change x to 10 and return (hard-coded) 3. Value of `sum` is definitely 5. x is a global variable and all three functions access same global x, (do not define local variable with the same name to overwrite global x). If a function is changing x, it is changing same copy of x that others access.

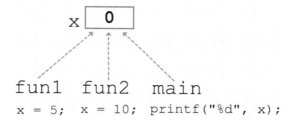

Both functions `fun1` and `fun2` are called in following statement

```
int sum = fun1() + fun2();
```

The two function calls are operands of plus(add) operator, if plus operator evaluate its operands from left-to-right, function `fun1()` is called first, setting the value of x to 5, then `fun2()` is called and final value of x is 10. Similarly, if order of evaluation of operands for plus operator is from right-to-left then the final value of x is 5.

> In C language, order of evaluation of operands for add operator (+) is unspecified.

What it means is that compiler is free to evaluate the operands from Left-To-Right or Right-To-Left.

Order or evaluation of operands is only defined for the following four operators in C language:

Operator	Name
&&	Logical AND operator
||	Logical OR operator
? :	Conditional operator
,	Comma operator

These operators are explained in great details in *Question 2.1*.

Question 2. 4: What is a NULL statement and where is it used?

A statement is either a **Simple statement**, or **Compound statement**. Each line in the following code is a simple statement:

```
printf("%d", 9);
x = area(2);
a = 5 + 6;
x++;
goto lbl;
```

All of them are simple statements. A semicolon, also called a statement terminator, is used to terminate simple statements.

A compound statement, also called a Block is a group of simple or compound statements enclosed within curly braces. A block has its own scope and it is not terminated by a semicolon. A semicolon (if exist) after a block is separate statements.

`if` statement below is followed by a compound statement that swap values of `less` and `more` using a temporary variable `temp`.

```
if(less > more)
{                       // Block start
   int temp = less;
   less = more;
   more = temp;
}                       // Block end
```

Each Block defines its own nested scope. Variable `temp` is local to this block and is not accessible outside this Block.

How you put opening braces depends on coding practice followed in your company. The most common ways are either to start the opening braces of a block at the end of current line

```
if( less > more) {
   ... ...   // BODY OF IF
}
```

of from the next line.

```
if( less > more)
{
   ... ...   // BODY OF IF
}
```

I prefer the second approach.

A statement can also be empty. Such a statement is called **null statement.** Both the statements below are null statements.

```
;  // A semicolon with no expression before it
{} // A pair of empty braces
```

A null statement is useful when language syntax requires a statement to be present but your code logic do not. For example, when `goto` label is put at the end of block as follows,

```
{
    ... ...
    {
      goto lblEnd;
       ... ...
    }
    lblEnd:
}
```

The code will not compile because `goto` label must be followed by a statement. We have to put a statement after it, even if it is a null statement.

```
{
    ... ...
    {
      goto lblEnd;
       ... ...
    }
    lblEnd: ;
}
```

Similarly, if entire logic to copy string `src` into string `dest` is written in condition expression itself. Then nothing is left to be done and we have to put a null statement in the body of loop as shown below

```
while(dest[i++] = source[j++])
    ;
```

or

```
while(dest[i++] = source[j++])
{ }
```

It will copy the null character also. There's nothing left to be put in body part, hence it is `null`.

Function `firstOcc` in Code 2.3 returns index of first occurrence of `ch` in string `str`

```
int firstOcc(char* str, char ch)
{
  int i=0;
  for (;str[i] != '\0' && str[i] != ch; i++)
    ; //null statement

  if(str[i] == ch)
    return i;
  else
    return -1;
}
```

Code 2.3

Even the following statements do not serve any purpose, but they may not be called null statement.

```
0;
(void*)0;
100;
```

Inside every function, control flows sequentially from top-to-bottom until branching or looping statement is encountered. Branching statements branch control to a particular point within the function either conditionally or unconditionally and Looping statements execute a statement (single or block) for some finite number of times or till a condition is satisfied.

No branching statement except `return` and function call (if you consider them branching statement) can branch the control out of a function.

Question 2. 5: What is conditional and unconditional branching.

Branching is transfer of execution control from one point to another within the program.

When control is transferred based on a particular condition it is called **conditional branching**, e.g. `if`, `switch`). When control is transferred without any condition it is called **Unconditional branching**, e.g. `goto`, `break`, continue, return and function call statements. Let us discuss them one by one.

if statement

if statement is used for decision making. It can be written either with or without else part as shown in *Table 2.2*.

if(expression)
    statement1
else
    statement2
	if (expression)
	    statement1

With else part	**Without else part**

Table 2.2

In both cases expression is evaluated for its boolean (integer) value, if it is true, statement1 is executed, else statement2 is executed (or nothing if else part is missing). statement1 and statement2 are executed in mutually exclusive way and no valid situation results in the execution of both of them.

Both statements are either simple or compound statement. We cannot have more than one statements in either if part or else part (multiple statements must be grouped into a block of compound statement).

expression must be enclosed within parentheses. Following code is an error because of missing parenthesis;

```
if x>0                    // ERROR
    printf("positive");
```

switch Statement

switch statement is used to conditionally branch, based on value of an integral expression. Syntax of switch statement is as follows:

```
switch(iexp)
{
    case ciexp1:
        ........
    case ciexp2:
        ........
        ........
```

```
case ciexpN:
   ........
default:
   ........

}
```

Code 2.4

`iexp` is an integral expression (switch expression) and `ciexp1, ciexp2 ...` `ciexpN` are constant integral expressions (case labels)[1].

Switch expression is an integral expression. Control is moved to the case label whose value is equal to the result of switch expression. If no case label is equal to value of switch expression and a `default` label is present, control goes to the `default` label. If no `default` label is present, control moves out of `switch` block.

Code 2.5 prints name of day corresponding to day number stored in `int` variable `day`.

```
switch(day)
{
   case 1: printf("Sunday"); break;
   case 2: printf("Monday"); break;
   case 3: printf("Tuesday"); break;
   case 4: printf("Wednesday"); break;
   case 5: printf("Thursday"); break;
   case 6: printf("Friday"); break;
   case 7: printf("Saturday"); break;
   default: printf("Not a valid day.");break;
}
```

Code 2.5

Following are some important points about `switch` statement:
- ✓ `switch` expression (`iexp` in Code 2.4) has to be an integral expression. Other types are not allowed.
- ✓ Case expressions (`ciexp1, ciexp2...` in Code 2.4) has to be constant integral expressions that can be evaluated at compile-time. These case labels are evaluated by compiler during compile time, therefore no variable allowed.

---

1. May include `sizeof`, cast to `int` and enumerations.

✓ A case or `default` label is accessible only within the closest enclosing `switch` statement.

✓ The compiler may implement `switch` statement as `if-else` or `goto`. But actual implementation is compiler dependent.

✓ `default` is optional and can be placed anywhere with respect to other case labels (not necessarily at the end).

✓ Though never useful, you can have statements in between the starting braces of `switch` block and first case label. It is unreachable code, but not an error. Following code is fine:

```
switch(crazyWish){
  int i=4;
  fun(i)
  case 0:
    i = 10; // Fall through into default
  default:
    printf("%d", i);
}
```

No matter what the value of case label (`crazyWish`) is, `fun` is never called, it is unreachable code[2]. Memory to `i` is allocated but, because of unreachable code, variable `i` never get initialized, and if `crazyWish` is non-zero, garbage gets printed.

✓ A `break` statement is used to move control out of `switch` block, `break` cannot move out of `if` or `else` block.

✓ Two case labels cannot have the same value and there can be only one `default` statement. Case label of a `switch` statement and another `switch` statement nested in it can be same. Following code gives compile-time error:

```
switch(x)
{
  case 2: ... ...
  case 1+1: ... ... // ERROR
}
```

---

2.   Unreachable code in C language is not an error. Following code is fine.
```
if(0)
    printf("Never Printed");
```
Some languages like java throw compile-time error for unreachable codes.

✓ The implementation may limit the number of `case` values.

Switch statement is used where we have options and different actions need to be performed for the different choice from users:

```c
int choice;
printf("choose from the output mediums: \n\t"
        "1. Console (default).\n\t"
        "2. File \n\t"
        "3. Printer.\n"
        "Your Choice : ") ;
scanf("%d", &choice) ;
switch(choice)
{
  default:        // Fall thru-default is console
  case 1: fnptr = stdout; break;
  case 2: fnptr = fp; break;
  case 3: fnptr = lpt1;
}
```

If `choice` is `4`, control moves to `default` and since there is no `break`, control fall thru `case 1:` and `stdout` is chosen.

Fall-thru is used when same action need to be performed for different values of `switch` expression. Code 2.6 count number of vowels and consonants in a string

```c
char inputStr[20] = "Ritambhara";
int cnt=0, vCount=0, cCount=0;

for(; cnt < strlen(inputStr); cnt++)
{
  switch(tolower(inputStr[cnt]))
  {
    case 'a':
    case 'e':
    case 'i':
    case 'o':
    case 'u':
      vCount++; break;
    default:
      cCount++; break;
  }
}
```

Code 2.6

The `for` loop can also be written as:

```
for(; cnt < strlen(inputStr); cnt++)
{
  ch = tolower(inputStr[cnt]);
  if( ch=='a' || ch=='e' || ch=='i' ||
     ch=='o' || ch=='u')
      vCount++;
  else
      cCount++;
}
```

It is possible that compiler internally converts `switch` statement to `if-else`, so there is no point arguing about which one is better, however a `switch` usually generates more compact code. Courtesy Sir Denis Rechie.

We could have merged the assignment to `ch` and `if` condition into one as follows:

```
if(tolower(inputStr[cnt]) == 'a' ||
   tolower(inputStr[cnt]) == 'e' ||
   tolower(inputStr[cnt]) == 'i' ||
   tolower(inputStr[cnt]) == 'o' ||
   tolower(inputStr[cnt]) == 'u')
```

But then function `tolower` is called 5 times in worst case, which is a (not so big) performance loss. By the same logic we should precompute the length of string

```
int length = strlen(inputStr);
for(; cnt<length; cnt++){
    ... ... ... ...
```

`switch` expression can be any complex expression as long as result is an integral value. For example:

```
switch (ch = getchar())
{
  default: putchar(ch);
           break;
  case 'Q': /* Quit Logic*/
}
```

`if` **statement v/s** `switch` **statement**

✓ `switch` can only be used with exact equality and not to make inequality decision (like `<`, `>`, `<=`, `>=`). Following code cannot be written using `switch`.

```
if( marks > 80 )
  printf("Excellent");
else if( marks > 60 )
  printf("Good");
else if( marks > 50 )
  printf("Average");
else
  printf("Poor");
```

However, every `switch` statement can be rewritten using `if`.
✓ Condition in `if` can compare two variables, but `switch` can only compare switch expression against compile-time constant case labels. Following `if` cannot be converted to `switch` because both are variables:

```
if( x == y )
```

✓ `switch` reduces the level of indentation and make the code more readable.
✓ And finally, we cannot use `break` to move out of `if` block.

Unconditional branching using `goto`

Brian Kernighan & Dennis Ritchi has written in their book
"C provides the infinitely-abusable `goto` statement, and labels to branch to."
Use of `goto` is refrained by structural programming guidelines because it makes program difficult to comprehend[3].

`goto` is used to transfer execution control from one point to another within the same function unconditionally. When `goto` is encountered, control of execution jumps to statement following `lbl:` (there must be a valid statement after label)

---

3. Donald Knuth selectively promoted the use of `goto` in his paper "structured programming using goto".

```
goto lbl;
   ...  ...
   ...  ...
lbl:
   ...  ...
   ...  ...
```

lbl is an identifier used as label. If lbl is not found, compiler gives an error complaining about undefined label in function. Following are some facts about goto:

✓ goto can transfer control only within the function. goto and the corresponding label should be in the same function block.

✓ Scope of a goto-label is the entire function and is not bound by inner blocks where it might be present. Following code is fine:

```
goto skip:
{
    int noUse = 3;
    skip:
    printf("%d", noUse);
}
```

initialization of noUse is skipped because control directly moves to printf, and value printed is garbage.

✓ Label cannot be the last thing in a block. It must be followed by some valid statement (even if it is null statement).

Everything that can be written using goto can also be written without it (goto is never recommended in structural programming) but there is a situation where goto can come really handy. When you want to jump out of nested loops, break can only jump one innermost loop, but goto can be used to jump out of entire structure.

```
while(...){
    ...
    while(...){
        ...
        goto out;
    }
}
out:
    ...
```

Question 2. 6: What is Dangling-Else problem?

In C language, when `if-else` statement is nested, then `else` is associated with the nearest `if`. Else part in `if-else` statement is optional. In the following nested `if` statement (I have intentionally not indented the code)

```
if(cond1)
if(cond2)
statement1;
else
statement 2;
```

There are two possibilities of associating `else` with the two `if`s.

1. Else with outer if	2. Else with inner if
`if(cond1)`	`if(cond1)`
`{`	`{`
`    if(cond2)`	`    if(cond2)`
`        statement1;`	`        statement1;`
`}`	`    else`
`else`	`        statement 2;`
`    statement 2;`	`}`

White spaces do not have any significance in the code. In a nested `if` statements, `else` is associated with the nearest unmatched `if` above it. For examples the following code:

```
if (doorIsOpen)
  if (residentIsVisible)
    greetResident("Hello!");
  else               // A "dangling else"
    ringDoorbell();
```

demonstrate the dangling-else problem, the same piece of code can be interpreted in two ways depending on which `if` gets the `else` instruction.

The problem is that both, outer `if` and inner `if` might conceivably own the `else` clause. In this example, one might surmise that `else` belong to the outer `if`, but C language associate `else` clause with the innermost `if` available (without `else`). The effective logic is as follows:

```
if (doorIsOpen)
{
  if (residentIsVisible)
  {
    greetResident("Hello!");
  }
  else
  {
    ringDoorbell();
  }
}
```

The dangling else grammar is inherently ambiguous and both C++ and Java has inherited the same from C. It's always good to write code with explicit braces indicating the associations clearly.

Question 2. 7: What are the different looping structures in C language?

There are three types of looping statements in C, for, while and do-while. They differ in either the ease of use in a given logic or point where loop-condition is put. for and while can be replaced with each other because both check the loop-condition before executing the body of loop. do-while checks the condition after executing body of the loop and is therefore useful in situations where statement (block) need to be executed at least once.

Following are the syntaxes of all the three loops along with their flow-charts:

While Loop

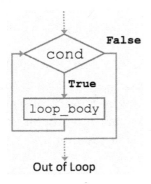

Out of Loop

```
while (cond)
  loop_body
```
Execute loop_body as long as cond is true. Ex. below while loop prints all characters entered by user until he enters an End-Of-File character (CTRL+Z).
```
while((ch=getch()) != EOF )
  printf("%c", ch);
```

If `cond` is always `true` then it becomes an infinite loop.

```
while(1){
   ... ... ...   // INFINITE LOOP
}
```

We are calling the above loop infinite but practically they may be terminated using a `break` statement placed inside the body of loop[4]. Following code will also print all characters till an EOF character is entered:

```
while( 1){
   ch=getch();
   if(ch == EOF )
      break;
   printf("%c", ch);
}
```

A `break` can only break out of nearest loop (`while`, `for` or `do-while`) or a `switch` block in which it is enclosed.

The `break` in the following code move execution out of the `while` loop and has no connection with the `if` block inside which it is actually present.

```
count = 0;
while(1){
   if(count == 10){
      break;
   }
   printf("%d ",count++);
}
```

The code print numbers `0` through `9` (post incrementing `count`). A `break` statement, if present, must be placed inside a valid block (either a loop body or `switch`) that it can break through. Following code is error.

```
main(){
   if(expr)
      break;   // ERROR. CAN'T BREAK FROM if
}
```

---

4.   Like in `switch`, `break` can also be used inside body of a `while` loop (or `for` or `do-while` for that matter) to move out of body of loop.

For Loop

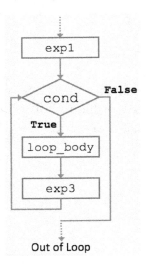

Out of Loop

```
for(expr1; cond; expr3)
    loop_body
```
expr1 (initialization) is evaluated only once. Then cond is evaluated, if it is false, control move out of the loop, else (true) body of loop (loop_body) and increment part (expr3) are evaluated in that order. cond is evaluated again and this process is repeated till cond becomes false.

expr1, cond and expr3 are all optional, default condition is true.

All the following four codes produce the exact same output:

1. Loop with all three parts:

```
for(i=0; i<n; i++)
    printf("Big-O");
```

2. Loop with two parts:

```
i = 0;
for(; i<n; i++)
    printf("Big-O");
```

3. Loop with only condition:

```
i=0;
for(; i<n; ){
    printf("Big-O");
    i++;
}
```

4. Loop without anything:

```
i=0;
for(; ; ){
    if(i>=n)
        break;
    printf("Big-O");
    i++;
}
```

Though not recommended, the code can also be written with empty body of loop as follows:

```
for(i=0; i<n; printf("Big-O"), i++)
    ;
```

Since, body of loop has to be given, null statement is used.

Do-While Loop

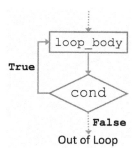

True

False

Out of Loop

```
do
    loop_body
while(cond);
```

do is a place holder indicating start of loop, loop_body is executed followed by checking of cond. Body of loop is executed till the cond is true.

In all the three loops, loop_body is a single or block statement.

break and continue

break and continue statements are Structural programming answer to goto statement. Both the statements transfer the control from one point to another unconditionally. But they have following structural programming restrictions.

break statement breaks out of body of the innermost enclosing loop or a switch statement block and move execution control to the statement immediately following the block (switch or loop).

continue can only be used inside a loop body (and not switch). It is used to skip executing rest of the loop_body in current iteration and move execution control to loop condition (in case of while and do-while loop), or increment part (in case of for loop).

Let us write a function that takes a string and prints all the characters in it except 'p' until it encounters character 'q' or end of the string[5]. For example,

```
Input String: Peter has a purple pen
Output: eter has a urple en
Input String: Action is eloquence.
Output: Action is elo

void printSpecial(char* str)
{
    do
    {
```

---

5.   Strings in C are implemented using char arrays and are always terminated by a null character.

```
    if(tolower(*str) == 'p')
      continue;
    else if(*str == 'q')
      break;
    else
      printf("%c", *str);
  }while(str++);
}
```

Code 2.6

Code above iterates on each character in the string, if that character is 'p' then skip the loop and continue to re-check the condition. If character is 'q', break from the loop without printing anything. For any other character, print it.

Question 2. 8: Which of the following two codes take more time?

```
for(i=0; i<10; i++)            for(i=0; i<100; i++)
  for(j=0; j<100; j++)           for(j=0; j<10; j++)
    printf("Hello");               printf("Hello");
```

First thing First! Both codes print Hello 1000 times and execute the body of inner loop same number of times.

In the first loop (left side), the outer loop executes 10 times and for each iteration of outer loop, inner loop executes 100 times. It means, for each value of i, j is initialized once and incremented 100 times.

In the second code (right side) for each iteration of the outer loop, inner loop is executed 10 times from scratch.

There are essentially four operations in each loop:
- **Assignment operations:** i=0 and j=0.
- **Increment operations:** i++ and j++.
- **Condition checking:** i<10 (or 100) and j<100 (or 10).
- **Print operation:** printf("Hello");.

We know that the printf operation is executed 1000 times in both the cases. Let us put counters for each of the four operations.

```
int main()
{
  int i, j;

  // COUNTERS
  int cnt1, cnt2, cnt3, cnt4;

  cnt1=0; cnt2=0; cnt3=0; cnt4=0;
  for(i=0, cnt1++; cnt2++, i<10; cnt3++, i++)
  {
    for(j=0,cnt1++; cnt2++,j<100; cnt3++,j++)
    {
      cnt4++;
      // printf("Hello");
    }
  }
  printf("Assignment: %d \nIncrement: %d \n"
         "Condition Check: %d\nPrintf: %d \n",
         cnt1, cnt2, cnt3, cnt4);

  cnt1=0; cnt2=0; cnt3=0; cnt4=0;
  for(i=0, cnt1++; cnt2++, i<100; cnt3++, i++)
  {
    for(j=0,cnt1++; cnt2++,j<10; cnt3++,j++)
    {
      cnt4++;
      // printf("Hello");
    }
  }
  printf("Assignment: %d \nIncrement: %d \n"
         "Condition Check: %d\nPrintf: %d \n",
         cnt1, cnt2, cnt3, cnt4);
}
```

Code 2.7

Output of Code 2.7 is

```
Assignment: 11
Increment: 1021
Condition Check: 1010
Printf: 1000

Assignment: 101
Increment: 1201
Condition Check: 1100
```

```
Print: 1000
```

From the above output, we can conclude that second code takes more time. As a rule, we can say that given a choice (if it does not change the logic), put the loop with less number of iterations as outer loop.

While searching in a two-dimensional array of order m*n linearly[6], traversing the array in row-major or column-major order does not matter in the logic.

Row-Major

```
for(i=0; i<m; i++)
   for(j=0; j<n; j++)
      if(arr[i][j]==data)
         return 1; // SUCCESS
return 0; // FAILURE
```

Column-Major

```
for(j=0; j<n; j++)
   for(i=0; i<m; i++)
      if(arr[i][j]==data)
         return 1; // SUCCESS
return 0; // FAILURE
```

If we know the structure of array, we can take advantage of it and alter the code accordingly.

Question 2. 9: How are the following two codes different?

```
int main(){                int main(){
  printf("Om");              while(1)
  main();                      printf("Om");
}                          }
```

See *Question 5.1*

---

6.   To learn about searching and sorting techniques read our book "Searching and Sorting for Coding Interviews".

Question 2. 10: Can we rewrite a for loop as while loop without distorting the logic?

The short answer to this question is, YES! In almost all the situations, a `for` loop can be replaced with `while` loop as shown in Table 2.3

```
for(expr1;expr2;expr3)            expr1;
{                                 while(expr2){
  loop_body                         loop_body
}                                   expr3;
                                  }
```

Table 2.3

Some may argue that the exact replacement may fail if `loop_body` has `continue`. For example, Code 2.8 prints `Om` 5 times, but Code 2.9 is an infinite `while` loop:

```
int main(){                       int main(){
  for(int i=0;i<5; i++){            int i = 0;
    printf("Om");                   while(i < 5){
    continue;                         printf("Om");
  }                                   continue;
}                                     i++;
                                    }
                                  }
```

Code 2.8   Code 2.9

But it is because of the blind replacement. If some thought is given, the `while` loop would have been written like:

```
while(i < 5){
  printf("Om");
  i++
  continue;
}
```

It will print `Om` 5 times and is exactly like the `for` loop. So whenever, we change the loop from a `for` loop to `while` loop (or vice-versa) we should give a conscious thought to `break` and `continue` statements inside the loop. After all, break and continue are unconditional transfer of control.

Question 2. 11: What is the output of following code?

```
for(int i=0; i<=32767; i++)
  printf("Om");
```

Now this is a tricky question, value `32767` is `215-1`. If your system is allocating two bytes memory to integer data type then its range of values will be from `-32768` to `32767` (i.e from `-215` to `215-1`). Normally integers are 4 byte long and the range is from `-231` to `231-1`. But, I think Turbo-C compiler still allocate only two bytes to integers.

Anyways, the point is that `32767` can be the maximum value an integer can hold. `i` being an integer will never be more than `32767` in that case. Hence, the condition in the `for` loop is always `true` and `Om` is be printed infinitely.

Question 2. 12: While comparing a variable with a constant (literal), which of the two comparison should be used ?

```
if( x == 2 ) …              if( 2 == x ) …
if( ptr == NULL ) …         if( NULL == ptr ) …
```

1. Variable == Literal   **2. Literal == Variable**

In first comparison, variable is on the left side of `==` and literal is on the right side. Whereas, in the second form we are writing the literal (`2`, `NULL`, and so on.) on the left side of `==`.

From point-of-view of performance and result, both are exactly the same. But, sometimes we accidentally write assignment operator (`=`) in place of equal-to operator (`==`). Compiler will not give error if we write:

```
if( x = 2 )
```

This condition is always `true`, because result of assignment, `x = 2`, is `2` (value assigned to variable), which is `true`. Similarly, assignment `ptr = NULL` is always `false` (`NULL` is pointer `ZERO`).

Most compilers give warning in such code, but such warnings may get lost in the other warnings. That's why I push for zero-warning code.

If we always put literal on left side of equality comparison then, when we write = in place of ==, it will be flagged as compile-time error.

```
if( 2 = x ) // Compile-Time ERROR.
```

We cannot assign to literals because they do not have lvalue. Developing a habit of writing the literals first may save some debugging time.

3.
POINTERS AND MEMORY

Question 3. 1: What is lvalue and rvalue?

When a non-register variable is defined, memory to that variable is allocated in data area or on stack depending on its storage class. There are three things associated with that memory:

1. An address (of either data area or stack).
2. A value stored in that address.
3. A name (variable-name) associated with that memory.

If `ivar` is an integer variable, defined as follows and memory allocated to `ivar` is at address `100`, then *Figure 3.1* shows the memory.

```
int ivar = 5;
```

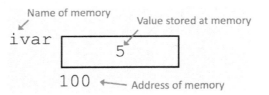

Figure 3.1

Address of memory (also called pointer) is the lvalue (pronounced as *"ELL-value"*) and value stored in that address is rvalue (pronounced as *"AR-value"*). Name of memory (`ivar`) can be used as either lvalue and rvalue, depending on the context.

Names lvalue (left-value) and rvalue (right-value) are given based on the side of assignment operator that an expression can come. e.g,

```
int x = 5;

x = 2; // x is lvalue, 2 is rvalue.
// y is used as lvalue below, x as rvalue
// x can be used as lvalue also as shown above.
```

```
int y = x;

// ERROR. 2 does not have lvalue
// cannot appear on left side of assignment
2 = x;
```

You can also think of lvalue as being "Locator-Value" and rvalue being "Value-of-Expression". Literals only have rvalue. In the following `scanf` command

```
scanf("%d", &x);
```

Ampersand operator (`&`) returns the address(lvalue) of its operand. It is compile-time error to apply `&` operator on operand that does not have an lvalue. Following expressions are lvalue expressions:

✓ A variable name.

✓ A subscript (`[]`) expression that does not evaluate to an array

```
arr[4] = 10; // arr[4] is lvalue expression.
```

✓ A member-selection expression (`->` or `.`)

```
// if head points to structure with field data
head->data = 5;        // head->data is lvalue.
```

✓ A dereference(`*`) expression that does not result in an array.

```
// if ptr is int pointer
*ptr = 5;              // *ptr is lvalue.
```

✓ An lvalue expression in parentheses

Note that array name is not an lvalue

```
int iVar = 3, arr[5];

arr = &iVar;    // ERROR. Array name is not lvalue
arr[0] = iVar;  // OK
```

But `arr` has an rvalue and can be used on the right side.

```
int *ptr;       // Pointer to integer
*ptr = arr;     // ptr points to 1st element of arr
```

Some authors talk about modifiable and non-modifiable lvalue. They say literals like 2, 'A',"Hello", 4.5, and so on. are rvalues. Array names and constant identifiers are non-modifiable lvalues and variables (objects) are modifiable lvalues. Even the standards lack consistency in defining them.

Kernighan and Ritchie coined the term lvalue to distinguish certain expressions from others, they wrote,

"An Object is a named region of storage; an lvalue is an expression referring to an object. An obvious example of an lvalue expression is an identifier with suitable type and storage class. There are operators that yield lvalues, if E is an expression of pointer type, then *E is an lvalue expression referring to the object to which E points. The name "lvalue" comes from the assignment expression E1 = E2 in which the left operand E1 must be an lvalue expression."

Initially, there was no rvalue in C. K&R decided that it's sufficient to just specify what expressions are lvalues and what expressions aren't. lvalue was required because language permits only lvalues in some contexts (e.g. operand of ++, --, & and left operand of =, -> and . operators). In other places, both lvalue and rvalue can come:

lvalues and rvalues got their names from their roles in assignment expressions, but, concept apply to all expressions. For example, x+1 results in an rvalue and hence the following assignment is error

```
x + 1 = 5;
```

lvalue expressions can also be complex, consider the following code:

```
int fun1(){
   int x = 3;
   return x;    // function returning rvalue
}
int* fun2(){
   static int y = 2;
   return &y;   // function returning lvalue
}

int main()
{
   fun1() = 5;   // ERROR. fun1() gives rvalue
   *fun2() = 5;  // OK. fun2() gives an lvalue
}
```

Code 3.1

Following statements are all errors, because left side is not lvalue:

```
++x = 3;  // ++x is rvalue
5 = 6;    // 5 is rvalue
(x+1)++;  // operand of ++ should be lvalue
(x+1) = 4;  // (x+1) is rvalue
```

Question 3. 2: What are pointers? How do we use them in C?

A pointer is an address in memory. Pointer variable is a variable that can hold memory address (like integer variable can hold an integer, integer pointer can hold address of an integer memory).

A pointer variable can hold address of only one type of memory and data type of a pointer is defined by the data type of memory whose address it can hold. An integer-pointer cannot hold address of a flo at memory (*Unless that address is explicitly type-casted to integer-pointer*). Definition of a pointer variable indicate its data type

```
datatype *variable_name;
```

Data type of memory   Name of pointer variable.
whose address this variable can store.

A memory address can be of code area, data area, heap area, or stack. Function pointers, that point to code area are little different and are discussed in *Chapter-4*. All other memory addresses can be assigned to data pointers.

Pointer Operators

To understand pointers, we must understand two operators, Address-of operator (&), and Value-at operator (*).

A pointer can only store address. Address-of operator (&) is used to get address of a variable in the memory. If we have an integer variable,

```
int ivar = 5;
```

and memory allocated to `ivar` is at address 100, as shown in the following screenshot:

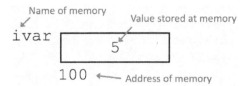

Then `&ivar` gives the address of this memory, i.e `100`. An integer pointer can store this address:

```
int *ptr = &ivar;
```

After this declaration (and initialization), memory looks as following:

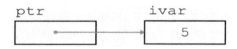

Because `ptr` is also a variable, it also has an address (`&ptr` = `200`). The value stored at memory allocated to `ptr` is of type integer-pointer (address of integer).

Actual addresses allocated to `ivar` and `ptr` may change with each execution. Therefore, addresses are not important, the fact that address of `ivar` is always stored in memory allocated to `ptr` is important.

```
ptr                 ivar
┌─────────┐       ┌─────────┐
│    •────┼──────▶│    5    │
└─────────┘       └─────────┘
```

`*` is value-at operator (Unary operator `*` is value-at, binary operator `*` is multiplication operator). It takes a valid memory location and returns value at that memory. `*ptr` should be read as *value-at-ptr*.

Table 3.1 shows the value of different expressions for `ivar` and `ptr` variables in previous example:

Expression	Value	Data type	Meaning
`ivar`	5	`int`	Value of `ivar`
`&ivar`	100	`int*` (int-pointer)	Address of `ivar`

Expression	Value	Data type	Meaning
`*(&ivar)`	5	`int`	Value at (Address of `ivar`)
`ptr`	100	`int*` (int-pointer)	Value stored in `ptr` memory
`*ptr`	5	`int`	Value at (`100`)
`&ptr`	200	`int**` (int-pointer-pointer)	Address of `ptr` (i.e. Address of address of `ivar`)
`*(&ptr)`	100	`int*` (int-pointer)	Value stored address of `ptr`.
`*(*(&ptr))`	5	`int`	

Table 3.1

The pointer declaration

```
int * ptr;
```

can be read as "value at `ptr` is an integer", indicating `ptr` is a pointer-to-integer.

Finding address using `&` operator is called Referencing, and finding value stored at an address using `*` operator is called De-referencing.

Variables declared as `register` cannot be referenced (cannot apply `&` operator on `register` variables), because they may not have a memory address. `void*` cannot be dereferenced as discussed in *Question 3.5*.

`*` has many meanings in C language, it is used as both multiplication and dereference operator. It is also used in declaring pointer variables. `*` in above declaration, can be placed closer to `ptr` or `int` or none. All the following declarations are same.

```
int* ptr;
int *ptr;
int * ptr;
```

We should prefer to stick asterisk with variable name because of its behavioural attachment with the variable. In declaration,

```
int * x, y;
```

x is an integer-pointer but y is an `int` variable (and not pointer). `int` in a declaration binds with all variables in the list but, asterisk (*) sticks only with the variable that follows it. In the following declaration

```
int x, * y, *z, p;
```

x and p are `int` but y and z are pointers.

As discussed earlier, an integer-pointer can only hold (unless explicitly typecast) address of an integer location. Following code is an error:

```
int iVar = 10;
char *chPtr = &iVar; // ERROR:Type mismatch.
```

Figure 3.2 demonstrate pointers; rectangular box shows state of memories after the statement(s) on left is executed.

Question 3. 3: Which operations can be performed on pointers?

We have already seen two pointer operators in previous question, Address-of and Value-at. They are called pointer operators, because they are used while dealing with memory, to find reference (address) of a variable and dereference a pointer.

Pointer arithmetic is performed on consecutive block of memory (usually an array). Following are the only arithmetic operations that can be applied on pointers:

1. **Increment:** Incrementing a pointer using ++ operator makes it point to the next block of memory (pointer incremented by sizeof data type that pointer points to).
2. **Decrement:** Decrementing a pointer using -- operator makes it point to previous block of memory (pointer decremented by sizeof data type that it points to).
3. Adding an integer to a pointer (+ or +=) moves it forward.
4. Subtracting an integer from a pointer (-- or -=) moves it backward by one memory.
5. Two pointers can be subtracted if they both point to elements in the same array.

```
void tryPointer(){
    int a = 10, b = 20, c = 30;
    int *p, *p;
```

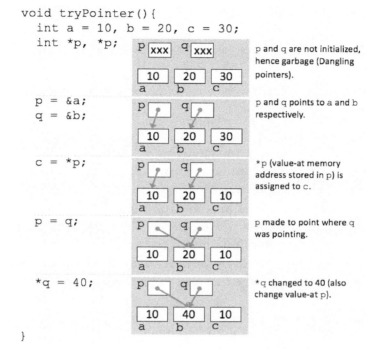

Figure 3.2

A pointer always moves in steps equal to the size of data type that it points to. If `sizeof(int)` is `4` and `sizeof(char)` is `1`, then a character pointer value is increased by `1` when incremented, and an integer pointer memory is increased by `4` when incremented.

```
int iArr[5] = {1, 2, 3, 4, 5};
char chArr[5] = {'A', 'B', 'C', 'D', 'E'};
int *iPtr = iArr;
char *chPtr = chArr;
```

Assume that memory allocated to `iArr` starts from address `100` and memory allocated to `chArr` starts from address `200`.

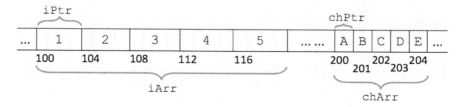

Value stored in `iPtr` is `100`, but `iPtr` points to memory block from address `100` to `103`. `chPtr` stores `200` and points to only one memory address. (`iPtr+1`) is `104` and (`chPtr+1`) is `201`. Following code prints all elements in an array `iArr`:

```
for(int i=0; i<5; i++)
  printf("%d ", *(iPtr+i));
```

In fact, compilers usually evaluate `iArr[i]` as `*(iArr+i)`.

If `iPtr` is incremented beyond the array boundaries, it may corrupt the memory in an unpredictable way. When pointer is not pointing to an array, arithmetic operations may not have any meaning.

When two pointers point to elements in the same array, then subtracting one from the other gives number of memory blocks in between them, and not the number of addresses between them. If there are two pointers, `ptr1` and `ptr2` pointing to the first and third elements in the same array,

```
ptr1 = &arr[0]; // ptr1 is 100
ptr2 = &arr[2]; // ptr2 is 108
```

then `ptr2-ptr1` gives `2`, number of integer memories between them and not the number of addresses between them (which is `8`). Result of the following expression is `8` because we are subtracting char-pointers.

```
(char*)ptr2 - (char*)ptr1
```

Question 3. 4: What are void pointers?

All data pointers, irrespective of their types, are allocated the exact same amount of memory (they essentially store memory address).

```
sizeof(int*) == sizeof(float*) == sizeof(char*)
```

Data type of a pointer is used while dereferencing it and using pointer arithmetic. If we have two pointers of different data types holding exact same address, then their starting point is same, but the size of block that they point to is different.

```
char *chPtr = (char*)&arr[0];
int *iPtr = &arr[0];
```

Both `chPtr` and `iPtr` store 100 in their memory. But when we dereference these two pointers, `chPtr` returns value stored at address 100 and `iPtr` returns integer value stored in memory block starting from 100 to 103.

A void pointer points to some memory without any knowledge of data type (and hence length) of the memory it is pointing to.

```
void *vptr;
```

Variable `vptr` can hold address of a memory location, but it does not have information about data type of that memory.

Without information of type of memory, we do not know length of memory and hence cannot dereference a `void` pointer and cannot perform any arithmetic on `void` pointers as shown in Code 3.2.

```
int main(){
    void *vptr;
    char ch = 'A';
    int ivar = 100;

    vptr = &ch;   //OK: Assign any pointer to void*
    printf("%c", *vptr); // ERROR: Can't dereference
    printf("%c", *(char*)vptr); // OK: print A
    printf("%d", *(int*)vptr);  // Print garbage
    vptr = &ivar; //OK: Assign any pointer to void*
    printf("%d", *vptr); // ERROR: Can't dereference
    printf("%d", *(int*)vptr); // OK: print 100
}
```

Code 3.2

Question 3. 5: What is Big-Endian versus Little Endian?

To understand big-endian and little-endian, we need to understand the memory (RAM). Consider memory as one large array containing bytes. In computer organization, people do not use the term "index" to refer to array locations instead, we use the term "address".

Each address stores one element of the memory "array". An element is typically (but not restricted to) one byte. If someone say that memory is byte-addressable, it is just a fancy way of saying that each address stores one byte. If we say memory is nibble-addressable, it means each address stores one nibble (4 bits = 1 nibble).

Size of integers is usually same as the word-size. If word on a machine is 32-bits long and machine is byte-addressable, integers are split into 4 bytes and each byte is stored in one address.

Consider a 32-bit number, 90AB12CD (each digit is hexadecimal digit. Since each hex digit is 4 bits, we need 8 hex digits to represent the 32 bit value). The bit representation of above number is:

```
1001 0000 1010 1011 0001 0010 1100 1101
```

The 4 bytes are: 90, AB, 12, CD. There are two ways to store this number in memory.

Big Endian

This format stores the most significant byte in the smallest address. Here's how it would look:

	90	AB	12	CD	
...	1000	1001	1002	1003	...

Little Endian

This format stores the least significant byte in the smallest address. Here's how it would look:

	CD	12	AB	90	
...	1000	1001	1002	1003	...

To remember which is which, recall whether the least significant byte (thus, little endian) or the most significant byte (thus, big endian) is stored first.

Consider a situation when you are sending data from a machine of one endianness to a machine of opposite endianness. You might not be able to determine the endianness of machine that sent the data. Just think about how you can solve it.

Endianness is reasonably well-hidden from users. If we do bitwise operations (e.g shift) on an int, we do not even notice the endianness. Machine arranges multiple bytes so the least significant byte is still the least significant byte (e.g., b7-0) and the most significant byte is still the most significant byte (e.g., b31-24).

Endianness does not apply on consecutive elements of an array. Address of arr[i+1] is physically sizeof(arr[i]) ahead of arr[i].

Code 3.3 has a function that check the endianness of a machine.

```
void checkEndian()
{
  unsigned int i = 1;
  char *cptr = (char*)&i;

  if (*cptr != 0)
    printf("Little Endian");
  else
    printf("Big Endian");
}
```

Code 3.3

Unix od command displays the file, byte-by-byte. It can be used to check the endian format of the file.

Endiness is more to do with architecture of the machine than with the individual file format. However, file format may be using it in a specific way. If a file format is dealing with individual bytes, then the Endiness of underline format actually does not matter (e.g. If the file is ASCII file).

Other file format may use specific Endiness format. For example, jpeg file format is big-endian, giff format is little-endian, whereas tiff format has the endian identifier encoded into the file and can handle both, for text file formats, the endianness does not matter.

Which one is better, Big-Endian or Little-Endian?:

Which one is better, Unix or Windows? Apple or Microsoft? Samsung Galaxy or iPhone? It's the same debate.

Question 3. 6: What is a memory leak and what are dangling pointers?

A pointer wrongly handled can be catastrophic, and that's an understatement. But surprisingly there are only two kind of errors in pointer programming, Dangling Pointers and Memory leaks. If we can get them fixed, we can champion the art of using pointers.

Memory leak

A memory leak is a situation when a memory is allocated to the program but it cannot be accessed. Such memory develops on heap, when we change the only pointer that holds the address of a memory on heap. Memory leak happens only in heap because memory on heap does not have a name.

```
int main(){
    int x = 5;
    int *ptr = (int*) malloc(sizeof(int));
    *ptr = 10;
    ... ... ...
}
```

x and ptr are local variables of main and are allocated memory in its Activation record. malloc function takes amount of memory to be allocated in bytes, allocate these many contiguous bytes on heap and return starting address of this block without initializing it. If sizeof(int) is 4

```
malloc(sizeof(int))
```

allocates 4 contiguous bytes on heap, we store the address of this memory in ptr. Now ptr points to a memory that does not have a name. The only way to access that memory is thru pointer ptr.

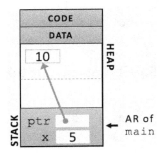

If `ptr` is assigned some other value, say, `ptr = &x;` then there is no way to access the memory on heap allocated to our program.

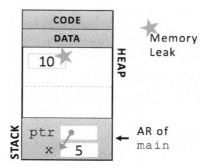

There is no way to use (or re-use) this memory. If total memory allocated is N bytes, 4 bytes out of it are lost. We are left with only N-4 bytes memory for our program. This is memory leak. If our program can run in N-4 bytes (which it should), we may not even notice the leak.

The most common way of getting a memory leak is by **reassigning the only pointer pointing to a heap memory**. In Code 3.4:

```
int *ptr;
for(int i=0; i<n; i++){
  ptr = (int*) malloc(sizeof(int));
  scanf("%d", ptr);
  printf("You entered : %d", *ptr);
}
```

Code 3.4

First iteration of loop allocates a memory and store its address in `ptr`. Next iteration allocates another memory and assign address of this new memory to `ptr` making the previous memory a leak.

That's like breaking the most important and obvious rule of the game. You must return the heap memory before the last pointer pointing to that memory is changed (and ideally as-soon-as you think you don't need it). If n is 1000, we have a memory leak equal to 999 integer memories.

When the memory on heap is no more required we must return it back to the available pool of memory using `free` function.

Another common mistake which lead to memory leak is when we do not `free` a pointer before it goes out of scope.

```
void func()
{
  int *ptr = (int*)malloc(sizeof(int));
  // do some work..
}
```

ptr resides in Activation record of function func. After func return, ptr no longer exist and memory pointed to by ptr becomes a leak. We must free the memory pointed to by local variables before returning.

```
void func()
{
  int *ptr = (int*)malloc(sizeof(int));
  // do some work..
  free(ptr);
}
```

What if there are multiple return points:

```
void func()
{
  int *ptr = (int*)malloc(sizeof(int));
  // do some work..
  if(Condition_1){
    return;
  }
  if(Condition_2){
    return;
  }
  free(ptr);
}
```

If function return from inside of any of the if conditions, there will again be memory leak. We should be cautious to free memory before the control can move out from any of the points.

```
void func()
{
  int *ptr = (int*)malloc(sizeof(int));
  // do some work..
  if(Condition_1){
    free(ptr);
    return;
```

```
    }
    if(Condition_2){
      free(ptr);
      return;
    }
    free(ptr);
}
```

Dangling pointers:

A dangling pointer is a pointer that points to an invalid object. We can have dangling pointers because of multiple reasons:

1. uninitialized locals

An un-initialized, non-static local pointer variable is a dangling pointer.

```
int * ptr;
```

ptr is a dangling pointer. They are also called wild pointers. Some languages (like Java) gives compile time error if you try to use uninitialized variables. Note that the following definitions are not dangling pointers:

```
static int *ptr;    // static are initialized
int *ptr2 = NULL;
```

As a thumb rule always initialize variables while defining them.

2. Pointing to out-of-scope variables

Another common way to get dangling pointers is when pointer points to a variable that has gone out of scope:

```
int *ptr = NULL;
{
   int temp = 10;
   ptr = &temp
}
/* temp goes out of scope and ptr is dangling beyond this
point */
```

3. Explicitly deallocating memory.

Once the memory is freed, if the pointer still points to that memory, then it is dangling pointer.

```
int *ptr = (int*)malloc(sizeof(int));
... ...
free(ptr); // ptr is now a dangling pointer
```

As a rule, always set the pointer to NULL after freeing the memory. The following two statements should always come in pair:

```
free(ptr);
ptr = NULL;
```

4. Side effect of deallocating memory

When a memory pointed to by a pointer is free, we should set it to NULL. This is to indicate that the pointer does not point to any memory now.
Sometimes, the memory is freed indirectly:

```
int *ptr = (int*)malloc(sizeof(int));
int *new_ptr = ptr;
free(new_ptr);
new_ptr = NULL;   // ptr becomes dangling
```

In above code, new_ptr is not dangling pointer. But since ptr was also pointing to the same memory, ptr becomes a dangling pointer because the memory to which it was pointing to is now deallocated.

5. Returning address of a local variable on stack.

```
int* func(){
   int abc = 5;
   return &abc; //return address of local variable
}
```

Variable abc resides on Activation record of function func. When func returns, this activation record is deallocated and address returned from function does not points to a rightfully allocated memory. The calling function will receive a dangling pointer.

```
int* func(){
   int abc = 5;
   return &abc; //return address of local variable
}
int main(){
   int *ptr = func();
   printf("%d", *ptr); // Prints garbage.
}
```

This problem is not there if the variable abc in function func is static.

```
int* func(){
   static int abc = 5;
   return &abc;
}
int main(){
   int *ptr = func();
   printf("%d", *ptr); // Prints 5.
}
```

Because static variables are not allocated memory in Activation records. They reside in the data area and do not cease to exist till the entire program is over.

Question 3. 7: How do you swap two variables without using a third variable?

This is a very common interview question, esp. at the junior level. Let us first write a function that swap two integers using a third variable.

```
void swap(int *a, int *b){
   int temp = *a;
   *a = *b;
   *b = temp;
}
```

Code 3.5

It must receive int* and not int, because we want to change the variables in calling function. In C++ variables can be passed by reference also,

```
// C++ Code. Won't compile for C language.
```

```
void swap(int &a, int &b)
{
    int temp = a; a = b; b = temp;
}
```

But C language does not permit pass-by-reference. It is easier to answer when the question is about swapping two integers. The question here is to swap two **variables**. A variable can be of any data type, either predefined or user-defined.

Before getting into these details, let us try to dissect popular answers,

Method-1: Using XOR Method

Using bit-wise XOR operator, two integral variables can be swapped without using third variable as shown in the following example:

```
X = X ^ Y;
Y = X ^ Y;
X = X ^ Y;
```

But XOR operator can only be used with integral data types (See *Question 2.1*). We cannot use this method to swap two floating point numbers of either single precession or double precession. Let us look at the next method

Method-2: Add-subtract method

The second method is using a combination of addition and subtraction operators, as shown in the following example:

```
X = X + Y;
Y = X - Y;
X = X - Y;
```

This method can swap two numbers of any type, but it is worse than previous method. If values of x and y are so large that their sum exceeds upper limit of their data type, then overflow happens. How C language handles overflow and underflow is not defined.

You may replace combination of add-subtract with multiply-divide, but problem of overflow is still there.

One limitation with both the methods is that they can only be used with predefined data types. They cannot swap two strings or even two pointers. In fact, even a code similar to Code 3.5 fails to swap two string. To swap two strings, we have to write a custom swap method as given in the following Code:

```
// str1 AND str2 ARE OF EQUAL LENGTH
void swap(char* str1, char* str2)
{
   int len = strlen(str1);
   for(int i=0; i<len; i++)
   {
     char temp = str1[i];
     str1[i] = str2[i];
     str2[i] = temp;
   }
}
```

Similarly, to swap two arrays or two objects of user-defined `struct` type, we have to write custom methods. While swapping user defined types, the complications of shallow-copy and deep-copy may also arise. There is no generic swap method that can swap two variables.

Now, you know what to answer, when an interviewer asks you to swap two variables without using third variable. With your answer, you may end up educating the interviewer.

Question 3. 8: What is a NULL Pointer?

According to the C11 standard, "*An integer constant expression with the value 0, or such an expression cast to type void*, is called a null pointer constant. If a null pointer constant is converted to a pointer type, the resulting pointer, called a null pointer, is guaranteed to compare unequal to a pointer to any object or function.*

Conversion of a null pointer to another pointer type yields a null pointer of that type. Any two null pointers shall compare equal."

What it means is that NULL is defined as `(void*)0`. It can be assigned to pointers when they do not point to anything. It is an indicative of the fact that the pointer is not garbage (dangling pointer), it is just not pointing to anything.

```
int *ptr; // DANGLING POINTER - GARBAGE
int *ptr2 = NULL; // NULL POINTER.
```

0 also represent NULL pointer and can be used in places where NULL pointer can be used. It is the only integer that can be directly assigned to a pointer.

```
int *ptr3 = 0; // NULL POINTER.
```

We need NULL pointers, to pass to functions as arguments when we don't have any valid pointer value to pass. We also need them to initialize pointers which are not pointing to any valid memory yet or which cease to point to a valid memory.

A pointer can be checked against NULL value.

```
int *ptr1, *ptr2, *ptr3=NULL, *ptr4=NULL;
if(ptr1 == ptr2){
   // MAY OR MAY NOT EXECUTE
}
if(ptr3 == ptr4){
   // ALWAYS EXECUTE.
}
```

Question 3. 9: What are `near`, `far` and `huge` pointers?

I was initially thinking of not putting this question in the book. What's the point of asking a question and then telling you that the question is not relevant any more? Companies no-more talk in the language of far and huge pointers, but some of our college teachers are not yet updated. So let us discuss them.

I searched the entire standard and could not find them, they are non-standard keywords with implementation-dependent behaviour.

It was relevant when CPUs used to have more RAM than the address space can point to e.g. 1 MB RAM with 16-bit address registers, that too on the Intel architectures. A near pointer was 16-bits long, while a far pointer and huge pointer needed to be big enough to hold complete physical address outside the current segment.

It was slower to compute the exact (segmented) address in far and huge pointers and for performance (both time and memory) reasons, near pointers were better.

Question 3. 10: How does `free()` function know the size of memory to be deallocated?

`free` is used to free the memory allocated using `malloc`, `calloc` or `realloc` functions on heap. Unlike `malloc`, `free` does not accept size of memory to be freed. If we have two pointers as follows:

```
int *iPtr = (int*) malloc(sizeof(int));
char *chPtr = (char*) malloc(sizeof(char));
```

then `free(iPtr)` frees 4 consecutive addresses starting from `iPtr`, while `free(chPtr)` only free the address stored in `chPtr`. It is left upto the compiler writers to decide how they want to implement this behavior.

One way, the compilers can handle this situation is, by allocating one word more than the space requested by `malloc`. This extra word is used to store number of allocated bytes that can be used later by `free()`.

Question 3. 11: What is the difference between `malloc`, and `calloc` functions?

Both `malloc` and `calloc` function are used to allocate memory on the heap. The memory allocated by both of them remains allocated unless explicitly deallocated or program terminates.

When successful, both functions return pointer to start (lowest byte address) of the allocated space. If memory cannot be allocated, both of them return a NULL pointer. When size of space to be allocated is zero, their behaviour is implementation defined.

The order and contiguity of storage allocated by successive calls to the `malloc`, `calloc`, and `realloc` functions is unspecified.

Following are the differences between `malloc` and `calloc`:

1. Signature

Signature of these functions is defined as follows:

```
void *malloc(size_t n);
void *calloc(size_t n, size_t size);
```

`malloc` only takes one argument, i.e. number of bytes, `calloc` takes two argument, number of blocks and size of each block.

```
malloc(n);
```

Allocates n bytes of memory. If allocation succeeds, a `void` pointer to the allocated memory is returned (that need to be type-casted to specific types). Otherwise `NULL` is returned.

```
calloc(n, size);
```

Allocates a contiguous block of memory large enough to hold n elements of `size` bytes each. The allocated region is initialized to zero. If allocation succeeds, a `void` pointer to the allocated memory is returned (that need to be type-casted to specific types). Otherwise `NULL` is returned.

2. Initialization

The memory allocated using `calloc` is initialized to zeros. `malloc` on the other hand does not initialize the memory it allocates.

We can achieve same functionality as `calloc` by using `malloc` followed by `memset`,

```
ptr = malloc(size);
memset(ptr, 0, size);
```

3. Faster

`malloc` is faster than `calloc`.

Question 3. 12: What is the use of `realloc` function?

`realloc` function is used to change the size of already allocated memory on heap. According to the `C11` standard, `realloc` is declared as follows:

```
void *realloc(void *ptr, size_t size);
```

The `realloc` function deallocates the old object pointed to by `ptr` and returns a pointer to a new object that has the size specified by `size`.

The contents of the new object shall be the same as that of the old object prior to deallocation, up to the lesser of the new and old sizes. Any bytes in the new object beyond the size of the old object have indeterminate values.

If `ptr` is a `NULL` pointer, the `realloc` function behaves like `malloc` for the given `size`. Otherwise, if `ptr` does not match a pointer earlier returned by a memory management function, or if the space has been deallocated by a call to the `free` or `realloc` function, the behavior is undefined. If memory for the new object cannot be allocated, the old object is not deallocated and its value is unchanged.

The `realloc` function returns a pointer to the new object (which may be same as a pointer to the old object), or a null pointer if the new object could not be allocated.

For example, following is an undefined behaviour:

```
int arr[2], i;
int *ptr = arr;
int *ptr_new = (int *)realloc(ptr, sizeof(int)*3);
```

And following is the right usage of `realloc`:

```
int *ptr = (int *)malloc(sizeof(int)*5);
int *ptr_new = (int *)realloc(ptr, sizeof(int)*3);
```

Question 3. 13: Write a function to check if the stack is growing forward or backward?

The most tempting and straight forward program seems to be

```
void stackDirection(){
  int first = 0;
  int second = 0;

  if(&second > &first)
    printf("Forward Direction");
  else if(&second > &first)
    printf("Backward Direction ");
}
```

We compare address of two local variables with respect to the point of their definition. If variables are allocated memory in the same order as they are defined in the code, then stack is growing in forward direction, otherwise it is growing in backward direction.

The fundamental problem in this approach is the assumption that variables are allocated memory in order of their presence in the code. i.e variable first is always allocated memory before second. Standard does not enforce this, and most popular compilers do not allocate memory linearly.

Even the storage on heap using successive calls to functions line aligned_alloc, calloc, malloc, and realloc does not guarantee the order and contiguity of storage allocated on heap.

Another provoking thought is to compare address of variables in Activation record of two different functions. It is guaranteed that when one function calls another, activation record of called function is put on top of activation record of calling function:

```c
void stackDirection(int *prev){
  int current = 0;

  if(&current > prev)
    printf("Forward Direction");
  else if(&current > prev)
    printf("Backward Direction ");
}
int main(){
  int local = 0;
  stackDirection(&local);
}
```

Code 3.6

But comparing two pointers is not a well-defined operation in C language. Pointer comparison with relational operators is not defined unless the pointers point to objects within the same array. Moreover, whether a stack exists or not, depends on the implementation. The ISO C standard does not mention the word "stack" even once.

Interviews are discussions, you do not have to justify anything, just put forward the facts.

Question 3. 14: Write code that accepts a string and print the following pattern; If the string is "RAM", then output should be

```
RAM
RA
R
RA
RAM
```

This question is put to better understand loops and nested loops. When we see a question, we should think of it as a problem that need to be solved logically, without getting into language syntax.

If length of string is n, first n lines are in one order (decreasing) and next n-1 lines are in another order (increasing). Let us have separate loops for these two. The following loop is supposed to print first n lines:

```
for(int i=0; i<n; i++)
{
   ... ...   // PRINT i'th LINE
   printf("\n");
}
```

We have not written the logic to print individual line. This loop will iterate n times and print new-line after each line. Now we need to see what to do in each iteration of the loop,

- when i is 0, print first n characters of string,
- when i is 1, print first n-1 characters of string,
- when i is 2, print first n-2 characters of string,
- ... ...
- when i is n-1, print first 1 character of string

Clearly, we need to print first n-i characters in string str. i.e.

```
for(int i=0; i<n; i++)
{
  for(int j=0; j<n-i; j++)   // PRINT i'th LINE
    printf("%c", str[j]);
  printf("\n");
}
```

This loop will print first n lines. To print the last n-1 lines, the outer loop will iterate n-1 times:

```
for(int i=1; i<n; i++)
{
  ... ...  // PRINT i'th LINE
  printf("\n");
}
```

In this case,

- when i is 1, print first 2 characters of string,
- when i is 2, print first 3 characters of string,
- ... ...
- when i is n-1, print first 4 characters of string

In each iteration, we should print first i+1 characters of string str.

```
for(int i=1; i<n; i++)
{
  // PRINT i'th LINE
  for(int j=0; j<i+1; j++)
    printf("%c", str[j]);
  printf("\n");
}
```

The complete program is given in Code 3.7

```
int main()
{
  char str[25];
  printf("Enter string:"); scanf("%s", str);
  int n=strlen(str);

  for(int i=0; i<n; i++)
  {
    for(int j=0; j<n-i; j++)
      printf("%c", str[j]);
    printf("\n");
  }

  for(int i=1; i<n; i++)
```

```
  {
    for(int j=0; j<i+1; j++)
      printf("%c", str[j]);
    printf("\n");
  }
}
```

Code 3.7

4.

ADVANCED DATA TYPES

Question 4. 1: How will you define a generic array that can hold all kinds of data?

An array is an indexed collection of homogeneous elements. All elements in an array has to be of the same type as given while defining the array. An array definition

```
int arr[5] = {1, 2, 3, 4, 5};
```

means all 5 elements are integers:

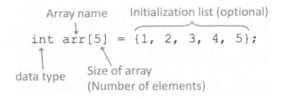

An array of void-pointers can be used as generic array as shown in the following code:

```
void* arr[3];

// MAKING ELEMENTS POINT TO DIFF. TYPE'S MEMORY
arr[0] = malloc(sizeof(char));
arr[1] = malloc(sizeof(int));
arr[2] = malloc(sizeof(double));

// STORING VALUES OF DIFFERENT TYPES IN ARRAY
*((char*)&(arr[0])) = 'A';
*((int*)&(arr[1])) = 10;
*((double*)&(arr[2])) = 5.3;
```

Code 4.1

The three array elements point to memory of different data types. In a way, this is generic array storing char, int and double data.

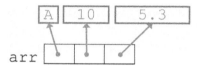

To dereference such an array, we need the information of data type that individual element points to.

```
printf("Element at arr[1] : %d", *(int*)arr[1]);
```

It can be argued that all the array elements are of exact same type, void*. C language does not have a true generic programming framework like polymorphism in C++. Macros are truly generic, but they cannot be used in this case and are also prone to errors.

Question 4. 2: What will happen if we partially initialize an array?

We know that, if array variable is load-time (global or static), it is initialized with zero by default. But an uninitialized automatic array holds garbage.

```
int main(){
    static int arr1[5]; // arr1[i] is 0.
    int arr2[5];        // arr2[i] is garbage.
}
```

If an array is explicitly initialized, each element is initialized with corresponding value given in the initialization list.

```
int arr3[] = {1, 2, 3, 4, 5};
```

If size of array is skipped, it is equal to number of elements in the initialization list. Size of arr3 is 5 integers.

If size of array is given and number of elements in initialization list are less than size

```
int arr4[5] = {1, 2};
```

then rest of the elements are initialized with zero. First two elements of arr4 are initialized with 1 and 2 respectively and rest with 0.

Arrays are never partially initialized.

This feature is used to initialize large arrays with zeros. All elements of an array of 1000 elements can be initialize to zeros in a single shot like the following:

```
int arr[1000] = {0};
```

Which is much more efficient than the loop

```
int arr[1000];
for(int i=0; i<1000; i++)
  arr[i] = 0;
```

Question 4. 3: How do you allocate array on heap?

`malloc` function does not know the type or nature of memory it is allocating, it just allocates a contiguous chunk of memory.

```
int *ptr = (int*)malloc(sizeof(int));
```

`malloc` function above has no information about the kind of data that will be stored in the 4 bytes of memory it is allocating (Assuming `sizeof(int) = 4`), whether it is used to store one `int` or an array of 4 characters. If we typecast this memory to `char*` and assign its address to a character pointer. It will be treated as an array of four characters.

```
int *chPtr = (char*)malloc(sizeof(int));
```

Remember both `ptr` and `chPtr` are not on heap. They are normal variables on stack holding address of memory on heap.

Irrespective of where array is (on stack, heap or data area):
✓ All elements are of same data type.
✓ All elements are allocated memory contiguously (and can be accessed using pointer arithmetic).

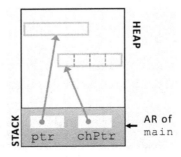

Memory allocated using `malloc` (or `calloc`) is also contiguous, we just need to reinterpret it as an array.

```
int main(){
   int arr[5] = {1, 2, 3, 4, 5}; // Array on stack

   // Pointer holds address of 1st element
   // Allocate 5 contigous integer memories on heap
   int *ptr = NULL;
   ptr = (int*) malloc(5 * sizeof(int));
   … … …
}
```

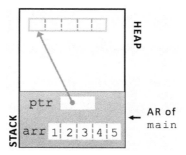

An array on heap cannot be initialized (*In C++ we can initialize the array on heap because new operator also calls constructor, where we can initialize, in addition to allocating memory*). If a pointer points to an array, it can access its elements like an array name (and vice-versa). If `ptr` points to first element of `arr`, the following expressions are the same:

Array	Pointer	Comment
`arr[2]`	`ptr[2]`	Access 2nd element of array
`*(arr+2)`	`*(ptr+2)`	Access 2nd element of array
`2[arr]`	`2[ptr]`	Subscript operator is commutative. Access 2nd element of array.
`*(2+arr)`	`*(2+ptr)`	Plus operator is also commutative. Access 2nd element of array.

Because of this property of pointers, while passing an array to a function, we pass only pointer to first element of the array (array name) and total number of element. The function that receives an array, receives it in a pointer variable (and not array).

```c
void printArray(int *a, int n){
    for(int i=0; i<n; i++)
        printf("%d ", a[i]);
}
int main(){
    int arr[5] = {1, 2, 3, 4, 5};
    printArray(arr, 5);
}
```

Output: 1 2 3 4 5

When function `printArray` is called, the picture of memory looks like the following diagram:

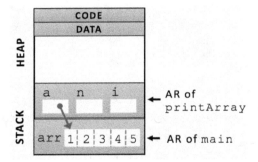

The array resides on activation record of `main` function only. If any change in an array is made within function `printArray`, it will change the array `arr` of `main`.

Array name (`arr`) has a special meaning. In most cases, it acts as a constant pointer to first element of the array. The following two codes compute sum of elements of array:

`int arr[]={1,2,3,4,5};`
`int iSum=0;`
`for(i=0; i<10; i++)`
`    iSum += *(arr + i);`
	`int arr[]={1,2,3,4,5};`
	`int iSum=0, *ptr=arr;`
	`for(i=0; i<10; i++)`
	`    iSum += ptr[i];`

2-dimensional array:

A 2-dim array can be thought of as an array whose individual elements are one-dimensional arrays. The memory allocation to a 2-dim array on heap is like this only. To accommodate a 2-dim array you need a pointer to `int` array (pointer-to-pointer-to-integer and not just pointer-to-integer).

```
int **p;
```

If an array is of 3*5 dimension (3 rows with 5 columns each). Memory allocation will be in two steps:

1. Allocate 1-dim array of 3 `int*` and store its address in `p`.
2. Allocate 1-dim memory of 5 integers, three times and store their addresses in `p[0], p[1]` and `p[2]`.

Following the code demonstrates this:
```
p = (int**)malloc(3 * sizeof(int*));
for(int i=0; i<3; i++)
    p[i] = (int*) malloc(5 * sizeof(int));
```

After memory allocation, memory looks like *Figure 4.1* (We have skipped the addresses but shown index of individual elements).

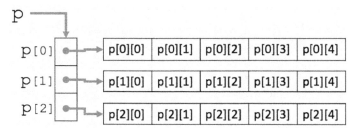

Figure 4.1

The array on the left side is an extra memory allocated. If this 2-dim array is on stack (`int arr[3][5]`) only 15 contiguous integers blocks of memory are allocated. But on heap

```
- 15 blocks of int memory location
- 3 blocks of int* memory location
- 1 int** memory location
```

While accessing `(i,j)`'th element of a 2-Dim array we have to derefer-ence both levels to reach the actual element. It can be done using any of the following methods:

```
p[i][j], *(p+i)[j], *(p[i] + j), *(*(p+i)+j)
```

The advantage of having a 2-dim array on heap is that each row can have different number of columns, as in figure 4.2:

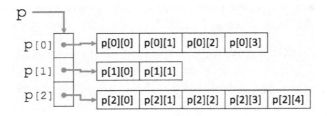

Figure 4.2

2-dim array on stack specifies number of columns in declaration

```
int arr[3][5];
```

We may end up wasting space in some unique situations. If undirected graph is implemented using adjacency matrix representation, the matrix is symmetric. Consider the graph and corresponding matrix in *Figure 4.3*

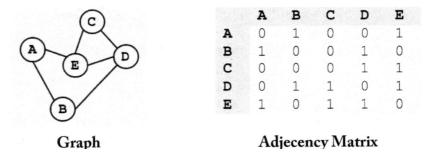

	A	B	C	D	E
A	0	1	0	0	1
B	1	0	0	1	0
C	0	0	0	1	1
D	0	1	1	0	1
E	1	0	1	1	0

Graph   **Adjecency Matrix**

Figure 4.3

There are ways to implement symmetric matrix that save space. Putting it on heap may not be the best way, but it is better than using a two-dimen-sional array.

N-dim Array

Arrays with more than two dimensions are difficult to visualize, but process of allocating them on heap remains the same with one more added level of abstraction. For example: The address of a three-dimensional array is `int***` and you need multiple loops as shown in Code 4.2.

Following is the C language code to allocate a 3-dim array of order A*B*C:

```
int ***p = (int***)malloc(A * sizeof(int**);

for(int i=0; i<A; i++)
  p[i] = (int**) malloc(B* sizeof(int*));

for(int i =0; i<A; i++)
  for(int j=0; j<B; j++)
    p[i][j] = (int*) malloc(C * sizeof(int));
```

Code 4.2

element at index (i, j, k) is accessed like `p[i][j][k]` or

```
*(*(*(p + i) + j) + k).
```

It can be further generalized for N-Dim arrays.

Deallocating 1-dimensional array

A one-dimensional array is a single chunk of memory allocated by a single `malloc` function call. It can be deallocated using a single call to function `free`.

```
free(ptr);
ptr = NULL;
```

The assignment of NULL to `ptr` is very important. It may otherwise make `ptr` a dangling pointer. Also, see that no other pointer should become dangling in this process. Consider the following code:

```
int *p = (int*) malloc(sizeof(int)*10);
int *q = p;
```

If we free the memory pointed to by pointer `p`

```
free(p);
p = NULL;
```

it makes q a dangling pointer, even when p is deallocated properly.

Deallocating 2-dimensional Array

To deallocate a 2-dim array in *Figure 4.1*, we have to first deallocate each element of the one dimension array on left (array pointing to arrays of integers) and then free pointer p that points to the 2-dim array

```
for(int i=0; i<m; i++)
  free(p[i]);

free(p);
p = NULL;
```

Note that if we first free p without freeing individual p[i], then all p[i]'s become memory leaks.

Note that we didn't assign NULL to individual p[i] elements. This is because they are deallocated in the very next statement.

Deallocating N-dimensional array

Deallocating a 3-dim array is intuitive generalization of the way we deallocate 2-dim array.

```
for(int i=0; i<A; i++)
  for(int j=0; j<B; j++)
    free(p[i][j]);

for(int i=0; i<A; i++)
  free(p[i]);

free(p);
p = NULL;
```

The process of deallocating memory is opposite to that of allocating memory. In C++, you may notice, the sequence of calling destructors is opposite to the sequence of calling constructors. While making a wall, you will first put the bricks and then apply plaster over it, while breaking it, you have to first break the plaster.

Question 4. 4: Is array name a pointer to type or a pointer to array?

Array parameters are passed to function as pointers and elements of array are also accessed using pointer arithmetic.

```
int arr[5] = {1, 2, 3, 4, 5};
```

In most cases, `arr` is address of first element and `arr[i]` can also be accessed as `*(arr+i)`. If integer-pointer `ptr` points to first element of array

```
int *ptr = &arr[0];     //OR JUST, int *ptr = arr;
```

then `ptr[2]` is exactly the same as `arr[2]`, clearly `arr` is acting as a pointer to `int`. However, `arr` itself cannot be changed. It is therefore a constant pointer to integer.

There are two situations in which array name acts as a pointer to the entire array and not just first element of the array:

1. **Operand to `sizeof` operator**: Operator `sizeof` on an array name gives size of entire array and not just `sizeof` a pointer (or first element). For example, `sizeof(arr)` is 20 (assuming 4 bytes for `int`). But `sizeof(ptr)` is equal to memory allocated to variable `ptr` in bytes and has nothing to do with what it points to.

2. **Operand to `&` operator**: When address-of operator (`&`) is applied on an array name, it gives address of entire array and not just the first element. If memory to `arr` is allocated as follows:

then both `arr` and `&arr` are 100, but `arr` is address of first element and `&arr` is address of an entire array.

`arr+1` points to next integer memory, i.e 104 but, `&arr+1` will move ahead by the size of entire array.

Question 4. 5: What are function pointers and how can they be used?

All the pointers we have seen till now are address of data memories (either in Stack, heap or data area). A function pointer is an address of function code (in the code area). If we have a function

```
int sum(int a, int b){ return a+b; }
```

then &sum is address of code of function sum. Function name also acts as a pointer to the function code, &sum and sum are same, both representing address of function sum at run-time.

Type of a function

For every data type (even user-defined data types) there is a type that is, 'pointer-to-that-datatype'. Declaring a pointer-to-integer, means declaring a variable of type int*. This int* is a data type used for pointers.

In C, a function is also a type. The type of function is determined by its signature (not including name of function and formal parameters). For example, type of both the following functions is same:

```
int sum(int a, int b){ return a+b; }
int product(int a, int b){ return a*b; }
```

The type is, "A function that accepts two integers and return an integer", and both sum and product are functions of this type:

✓ sum is a function that accepts two integers and return an integer.
✓ product is a function that accepts two integers and return an integer.

A pointer variable that can hold address of sum or product (or other functions of the same type) should be defined as a pointer-to-a-function-that-accepts-two-integers-and-return-an-integer. ptr is such a pointer.

```
int (*ptr)(int, int);
```

To understand this definition, start the from the variable name and proceed as per precedence rules:

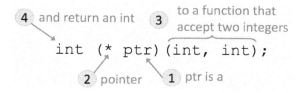

We can call the function pointed to by `ptr` (dereference `ptr`) using normal function call operator:

```
ptr = &sum;         // ptr POINTS TO FUNCTION sum
int x = (*ptr)(2, 3);     //CALLING sum

ptr = product;      // ptr POINTS TO FUNCTION product
x = ptr(2, 3);            // CALLING product
```

Both the following function calls are exactly same and valid:

```
(*ptr)(2,3);
ptr(2,3);
```

Each element of the following array, `arr` can hold a pointer to function that accept two integers and return an integer (same as `sum` or `product`).

```
int (* arr[2])(int, int);
```

`arr` is an array of two elements, each of which is a pointer to function that accepts two integers and return integer. Read this declaration starting from `arr`, following the precedence rule, as shown in the following figure:

```
4 and return an int      3 to a function that accept two integers
    int (* arr[2])(int, int);
                    1 arr is an array of two elements
          2 Each of which is a pointer
```

Use `typedef` to make good reading:

```
typedef int (*FP_TYPE)(int, int);

FP_TYPE getFunction(const char ch){
```

```
switch(ch){
   case '+': return sum;      break;
   case '*': return product; break;
   ... ...
  }
}
int main(){
  FP_TYPE funPtr;
  funPtr = getFunction('+');
  printf("%d", funPtr(2, 3)); // CALLS sum
}
```

Output: 5.

Complicated declarations

The way to read complicated declarations is same as above, start from the name and go as per precedence rule. Let us look at some declarations

Declaration	Comment
`int P()`	P is a function that returns `int`.
`int * P()`	P is a function that returns `int*`. (precedence of function call is more than value-at, read `P()` before `*P`).
`int (*P)()`	P is a pointer to function that returns `int`.
`int (*P)(char*)`	P is a pointer to function that accepts `char*` and returns `int`.
`int (*p())[2]`	P is a function that returns a pointer to array of 2 elements which are `int`.

Functions pointers are used to achieve dynamic-binding (run-time binding) in C language. The actual function called is determined at run-time,

```
int arr[n];
... ... ...
if(n<1000)
  ptr = insertionSort;
else
  ptr = quickSort;
... ... ...
```

```
ptr(arr, n);
```

Actual function called above depends on the number of elements in array. When elements are less, call insertion sort else quick sort.

C++ use function pointers internally to implement virtual functions. There are some basic differences between function-pointers and normal data-pointers.

1. Cannot allocate or deallocate memory to function pointers.
2. Unlike normal pointers, a function pointer points to code area.

Question 4. 6: Can we declare array of any type?

We cannot have an array whose individual element is of type `void`. Following code is an error:

```
void arr[5]; // ERROR
```

This is probably because it is impossible to determine the amount of memory to be allocated to `arr`.

We cannot have an array of function type also, and following statement is also an error:

```
int (arr[2])(int, int); // ERROR
```

However, array of both void-pointers and function-pointers are valid.

```
Void* arr[5]; // OK
int (* arr[2])(int, int); // OK
```

Question 4. 7: Can we have a variable length array?

Before C99, it was not allowed to declare arrays with variable length.

```
int n = 10;
int arr[n]; // ERROR BEFORE C99
```

Support for variable length arrays came in C99. Many compiler writers, esp. Microsoft, were lazy in incorporating this particular change. So are many authors, who continue to write, variable length arrays are not allowed in C till as late as 2004, after that I stopped reading those authors.

The fact is that automatic arrays in C language can have variable length. Global and static arrays must be of constant length.

```
int n = 10;
int arr[n]; //ERROR

int main(){
    int m=10;
    static int arr2[m]; // ERROR
    int arr[m];         // OK
    return 0;
}
```

We can also use variable-length arrays as arguments to functions:

```
void fun(int len, char data[len]);
```

Arrays declared as struct fields should have a fixed length, some compiler-extensions allow variable length arrays as struct fields.

Question 4. 8: How do we pass 2-dim arrays to function?

While passing one dimensional array to a function, we pass address and number of elements separately.

```
int func(int *arr, int n){ ... ... }
```

Even if we mention empty brackets, it means the same

```
int func(int arr[], int n){ ... ... }
```

But only first dimension can be left like this, all other dimensions has to be specified explicitly. The following code is an error:

```
int func(int arr[][], int n, int m){ ... ... } // ERROR
```

If we mention the second dimension, then it is fine:

```
int func(int arr[][5], int n){ ... ... }
```

The second dimension has to be specified. There are two popular ways of passing a multi-dimensional array to function

First is when dimensions are available globally, either as macro, constant or variable.

```
#define N 4
```

```
#define M 5

void fun(char data[N][M]);
```

As stated above, the first dimension can be skipped. Second way is to pass size as function parameter.

```
int func(int n, int m, int arr[n][m]){ … … }
int func(int m, int arr[][m]){ … … }
```

This is variable length array, needless to say, variable length arrays work only if your compiler is compatible with C99 standard.

In some specific cases, we can also pass two-dim array typecast as one dimensional and receive it in a single pointer array as shown in Code 4.3.

```
void printArray(int *arr, int m, int n){
  int i, j;
  for (i = 0; i < m; i++){
    for (j = 0; j < n; j++)
      printf("%d ", *((arr+i*n) + j));
    printf("\n");
  }
}
int main(){
  int arr[][3]={{1, 2, 3}, {4, 5, 6}, {7, 8, 9}};
  printArray((int *)arr, 3, 3);
  return 0;
}
```

Code 4.3

We are just reinterpreting the 2-dim array as one-dim chunk of memory and take advantage of its contiguous memory allocation.

Can we do the same for two dimensional arrays allocated on heap? NO !

Question 4. 9: How is `strlen` different from `sizeof`?

Strings are null terminated character arrays. A special format specifier, `%s` is dedicated for reading/writing strings. Strings are declared as character arrays only.

```
char str[10];
```

The difference is that `str` can only hold upto 9 characters (because last space should be left for null character).

There are two lengths associated with a string, size of memory allocated (to the array) and length of string stored in that memory.

```
char str[10] = "Hello";
```

```
str | H | e | l | l | o | \0 |   |   |   |   |
        _____/
            strlen(str)
      _____/
                  sizeof(str)
```

10 character memory is allocated to `str`, but it stores a string of length 5 only. `sizeof(str)` return length of memory in bytes allocated to `str`, in this case 10. `strlen(str)` is a library function to find length of string stored in memory of `str`.

```
printf("%d : %d", sizeof(str), strlen(str));
```

Output: 10 : 5

Another difference is, `sizeof` is an operator and `strlen` is a function. `sizeof` is a unique operator that is applied at compile time, it means, output of `sizeof` can be used to initialize load-time variable, but output of `strlen` cannot.

```
static int x = sizeof(str);      // OK. X = 10
static int y = strlen(str);      // ERROR.
```

The second statement is error because load-time variables cannot be initialized with return value of a function (See *Question 1.3*).

Result of `sizeof` on a string will always be same, but, `strlen` may change when the string value change.

```
char str[10] = "Hello";
printf("\n%d : %d", sizeof(str), strlen(str));

strcpy(str, "Bye");
printf("\n%d : %d", sizeof(str), strlen(str));
```

Output:
```
10 : 5
10 : 3
```

Question 4. 10: Can I use `sizeof` on array parameters?

We know that arrays are passed as pointers. The formal parameter that accepts array is a pointer, if `sizeof` is applied on that pointer, it will give number of bytes allocated to that pointer and not the size of array.

There is no direct way to find size of an array inside the function that receives it. That's why we have to pass it explicitly as extra parameter.

Question 4. 11: Implement `strcpy` function.

The signature of `strcpy` function is as follows:

```
char *strcpy(char *dest, const char *src);
```

It copies string pointed to by `src`, including the terminating `null` character (`'\0'`), to string pointed to by `dest` and returns a pointer to the destination string.

The responsibility of ensuring that destination string (`dest`) is large enough to receive source string (`srs`) and the two does not overlap rests with the calling function. Implementation of `strcpy` is shown in Code 4.4.

```
char * myStrcpy(char *dest, char *src)
{
   while(*dest++ = *src++);   // NULL LOOP BODY
   return dest;
}
```

Code 4.4

Question 4. 12: Write a function to swap two strings.

Sometimes we tend to write the below function

```
void swap(char *str1, char *str2){
   char *temp = str1;
   str1 = str2;
   str2 = temp;
}
```

This function swaps two local pointers and not the two strings. If the function is called as follows:

```
int main(){
   char s1[15] = "Ritambhara";
   char s2[15] = "Technologies";
   swap(s1, s2);

   printf("s1: %s | s2: %s", s1, s2);
}
```

Output: s1: Ritambhara | s2: Technologies

When swap function is called, the memory looks like *Figure 4.4*.

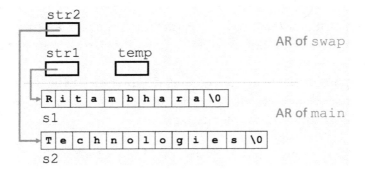

Figure 4.4

Function swaps local variables str1 and str2, but content of s1 and s2 remains unchanged. The way to swap two strings is to individually swap each character. If both strings are large enough to store the other, Code 4.5 swaps the two string,

```
void swap(char *str1, char *str2){
   bool charInStr1 = (*str1 != '\0');
   bool charInStr2 = (*str2 != '\0');
```

```
for(;charInStr1 || charInStr2; str1++, str2++){
  char temp = *str1;
  *str1 = *str2;
  *str2 = temp;
  if(*str1 == '\0'){
    charInStr1 = false;
  }
  if(*str2 == '\0'){
    charInStr2 = false;
  }
}
}
```

Code 4.5

Question 4. 13: What is wrong in Code 4.6 below?

```
char* getString(int n){
  char str[n];
  return str;
}
```

Code 4.6

The problem with this code is same as discussed in *Question 3.6*. String str is a local variable in activation record of function getString on the Stack. By the time control reach the calling function, str is deallocated and pointer becomes dangling pointer.

As a thumb rule we should never return address of auto variables from a function. There are two ways to resolve this issue, one is to define the string str as static. It will be allocated memory in data area and its address will remain valid even after deallocation of function's activation record.

```
char* getString(int n){
  static char str[n];
  return str;
}
```

Another way is to allocate string on heap. Memory to heap remain allocated till it is explicitly deallocated.

```
char* getString(int n){
  char *ptr = (char*)malloc(sizeof(char)*n);
  return ptr;
}
```

Responsibility of deallocating this heap memory rests with the calling function.

Question 4. 14: How do you find the size of a structure type without using `sizeof` operator on the structure (you can apply `sizeof` on individual fields)?

You may be tempted to calculate the size of individual fields of structure and add them to get size of structure. If struct ABC is defined as:

```
struct ABC{
  char ch;
  int x;
  char ch2;
};
```

You may say that

```
sizeof(ABC) = sizeof(char) +
              sizeof(int) +
              sizeof(char);
```

But there is a problem in this approach, a padding (extra memory) may be added after individual fields of structure objects to align them with word boundary in order to optimize the read/write operations. For example, if memory word size is 4 bytes, the above structure may take 12 bytes of memory even when sizeof(char) is 1 and sizeof(int) is 4.

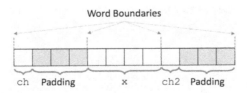

Figure 4.5

Gaps in the structure memory are marked as grey in *Figure 4.5*. Out of 12 bytes of memory allocated to the structure, only 6 bytes are used to store the actual data, the other 6 bytes are used as padding to align other fields with word boundary. Usually, characters do not need padding before them.

If the fields of the same structure are rearranged, it may take less memory.

```
struct ABC_LESS_PADDING
{
    char ch;
    char ch2;
    int x;
};
```

Memory allocated to objects of above structure is

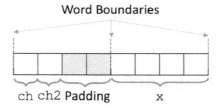

Word Boundaries

ch ch2 Padding   x

> Size of a structure may not be equal to sum of size of individual fields of the structure.

Coming to the original question, **size of a structure cannot be computed like this**. If we do not want to apply `sizeof` operator directly on structure, we can still find size by allocating an array of that structure type and finding difference in address of consecutive array elements.

```
struct ABC arr[2];
printf("Size of Structure : %d",
        (char*)&arr[1] - (char*)&arr[0]);
```

Typecasting to `char*` is required. The value of `&arr[1]-&arr[0]` is one because memory difference is always computed for the type of memory.

This way we can find size of any date type. As we know `sizeof` is applied at compile time, we can use above method to find size of any data type at run-time.

The following macro can be used to compute size of object of any type, `T`

```
#define SIZE(T)  (char*)(&T + 1)-(char*)(&T)
int main(){
    int x;
    printf("%d", SIZE(x));
}
```

But this macro cannot compute size of type directly (without any variable), `SIZE(int)` gives error at compile-time.

Question 4. 15: Can we have a structure field of the same `struct` type like below?

```
struct Node
{
  int x;
  struct Node y;
};
```

For sake of argument, let us assume that such a declaration is allowed. When variable of above structure type is defined.

```
struct Node var;
```

The memory allocated to `var` has two parts, one integer memory and one memory of type `Node` which in turn has `x` and `Node,` and so on. If this type of definition is allowed, then variables of such a type of structure requires infinite memory.

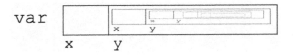

But can we have a field that is pointer to the same structure type as shown in the following code?

```
struct Node
{
  int x;
  struct Node *y;
};
```

It is allowed because all the pointer variables take fixed amount of memory irrespective of their type. If `int*` take 4 bytes, then `struct Node*` also take 4 bytes only. Hence memory to such structure variables can be easily allocated:

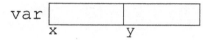

Such a structure, with one data field and a pointer pointing to the structure of same type form basis of dynamic data structures like linked list and binary trees.

Question 4. 16: What are dynamic arrays?

First a disclaimer, Dynamic Array is not dynamically allocated array. They are those arrays whose size can change dynamically at run time. For example, if initial size is 10, then if and when required, the size becomes 20 or even more.

Even if array is allocated on heap (dynamically allocated) like

```
int *arr = (int*) malloc(10*sizeof(int));
```

the size of this array is fixed (to be 10) and cannot change while the program is executing.

Static sized arrays

When we define arrays as follows

```
int arr[100];
```

size of array is fixed at compile time. Such arrays are called statically sized arrays or simply static arrays.

Variable length arrays

The length of an array (since C99) is allowed to be a variable.

```
int n;
scanf("%d", &n);
int arr[n];
```

The value of n is known only at run time. At compile time, this value is not known. But even in this case, size is fixed when array is allocated memory. If n is 10, then the size of array is 10 and remains 10 even if n changes. In next execution, size can be different, but for this execution it will be 10 only.

It is different from static arrays, because size is not fixed at compile time and may be different for successive executions.

In all the cases above (array on heap, statically sized arrays and variable length arrays), size of array, once allocated, cannot be changed.

Dynamic Arrays

Consider a use case, where array holds different number of elements at different point of time in execution. For example, during 80% of execution time, array stores 100 elements but sometime, it is required to hold 10000 elements. Then there are two options:

1. Define an array of size 10000 (max usage). 80% of time, only 1% of total memory available in the array is actually used. This is a huge wastage of memory.
2. Use Linked list. This optimize memory usage but there are other problems:

   a. Accessing an element in list is O(n) time operation and not O(1) time, as in arrays.
   b. For each element, an extra pointer is allocated. We may end up allocating more memory than array if data type is primitive (like char, that takes much less memory than a pointer).
   c. Binary search is not possible in linked list and sorting may not be as easy (*For Searching and sorting and their applicability on different data structures, read, "Searching and Sorting for Coding Interviews"*).

Another solution is to use Dynamic Arrays. In C++ and Java, dynamic arrays are implemented as `Vector` and `ArrayList` respectively. The approach is as follows:

Initially allocate an array of size X, say, X=16. As long as the number of elements are less than 16 continue to use this array. When number of elements become equal to 16, allocate a new array of size, say 32, copy elements from this array to the new one and deallocate previous array. Now array pointer is pointing to new array and we continue to use this one till number of elements does not exceed 32.

The class that implement dynamic array has following properties:
- ✓ Pointer pointing to array on heap.
- ✓ **Size:** Number of elements currently in the array.
- ✓ **Capacity:** Max number of elements that can be stored (>size).

And it exposes following methods:
- ✓ `Get(i)`: return element at i'th index in the array. O(1) time.
- ✓ `Set(i, val)`: set element at i'th index to `val`. O(1) time.
- ✓ `InsertAtEnd(val)`: Insert element `val` at the end of array. usually O(1) but can take O(n) time
- ✓ `Remove(i)`: Remove element at index i. O(n) time.
- ✓ `Size()`: return number of elements in the array.

5.
FUNCTIONS AND FILE HANDLING

Question 5. 1: What is the difference between 'infinite loop' and 'infinite recursion'?

Let us compare the following two codes:

```
int main(){                 int main(){
  while(1)                     printf("Hello");
    printf("Hello");           main();
}                           }
```

1. Infinite Loop   **2. Infinite Recursion**

First code is an infinite loop and keep printing Hello infinitely. It has to be force stopped (by killing the process).

Second code calls main recursively and in each function call, Hello is printed once. It is an unconditional recursion without any terminating condition.

Effectively, both codes are printing Hello and there is nothing to stop their execution. Difference is in the memory foot prints of these two codes.

In first code, main function is called only once and only one activation record is created. The memory usage remains constant and does not change with time. In second code, main calls itself again creating a new activation record on top of Stack. Every time main calls itself, memory consumption increases. Memory keeps increasing with time, and eventually, there is no space left that can be allocated to next function call of main. The memory-stack-overflows and program crash. *Figure 5.1* shows memory image of two codes.

I know a developer manager whose favourite interview question is, *"In how many different ways can you crash the program?"*

We just saw one way of doing that. Another, more obvious way is to generate an exception (like divide-by-zero) at run time. Yet another way to crash a program is to allocate lot of memory on heap, so that no space is left for stack to grow as shown in Code 5.1

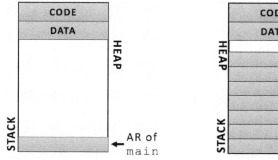
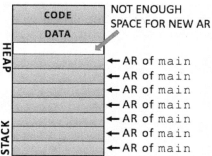

1. Infinite Loop   **2.Infinite Recursion**

Figure 5.1

```
int main()
{
  int *ptr;
  do{
    ptr = (int*)malloc(sizeof(int));
  }while(ptr != NULL);
  main();
}
```

Code 5.1

The while loop keeps allocating memory on heap and create memory leaks till there is space. It breaks out of loop only when it is not able to allocate any memory. Because heap and stack shares same memory, there is no room left for stack to grow. No new activation record can be created and program crash when a function is called (main called recursively).

Question 5. 2: Print Hello n times without using a loop?

If we are allowed to use a loop, then it is straightforward:

```
void printHello(int n){
  for(int i=0; i<n; i++)
    printf("Hello");
}
```

In most cases, recursion is a replacement of a loop where function does what body of the loop is doing.

```
void printHello(int n){
  if(n > 0){
    printf("Hello");
    printHello(n-1);
  }
}
```

This function need to be called like:

```
int main(){
  printHello(10);
}
```

As seen in previous question, recursive code takes more time than a loop.

Question 5. 3: What are static functions in C?

Functions in C language are global and have same kind of linkage as global variables. We cannot define a local function nested within another function. When a function (or global variable) is defined as static, their access is restricted to within the same file in which they are defined.

Static functions and static global variables are private within a file. This way, we can have two functions with same name in two different files within same program.

Question 5. 4: How can a function return multiple values?

A function can only return one value from the return statement directly, but indirectly, it can return multiple values by populating local variables of calling function whose address is passed to it as parameters.

Consider an example, Code 5.2 shows Linked-list implementation of stack that can hold only non-negative values.

```
// Node of Linked list implementation of Stack
```

```c
typedef struct node{
  unsigned int data;
  struct node* next;
}Node;

// Points to the head (top) of stack.
Node *top = NULL;

int isEmpty(){
  return (NULL == top);
}

int pop(){
  if(isEmpty())
    return -1;
  else{
    // DELETE THE NODE AT HEAD
    unsigned int retValue = top->data;

    Node* temp = top;
    top = top->next;
    free(temp);

    return retValue;
  }
}

bool push(unsigned int v){
  Node* temp = (Node*)malloc(sizeof(Node));

  if(NULL == temp) // UNABLE TO ALLOCATE
    return false;

  // INSERTING AT HEAD OF LIST
  temp->data = v;
  temp->next = top;
  top = temp;

  return true;
}
```

Code 5.2

push function inserts a new node at the head and pop removes the first node and returns its value giving a Last-In-First-Out arrangement.

When stack is empty, pop function returns -1. It is because of this reason why return type of pop is int and not unsigned int, because same return statement that returns value is also used to pass information of empty stack.

We may want to return two values in pop, actual value poped, and a boolean value indicating whether or not the stack is empty. Code 5.3 does exactly that:

```
bool pop(unsigned int * retValue){
  if(isEmpty())
    return false;    // retValue IS NOT SET
  else
  {
    *retValue = top->data;

    Node* temp = top;
    top = top->next;
    free(temp);

    return true;    // retValue IS SET
  }
}
```

Code 5.3

When return value is true, popped value is stored at address passed to this function (in retValue) else, it remains unchanged.

Question 5. 5: What is the output of below printf function?

```
int x = 5;
printf("%d %d ", x++, x++);
```

If you are reading this answer, then you have not read this book carefully, it was discussed while discussing comma operator in *Question 2.1*.

The order of evaluation of function parameters is undefined.

Question 5. 6: What is the signature of main function?

main is the function that is called at program startup. This function does not require any prototype and return type of main is int. We have not included `return` statement in `main` function in this book to save space. We encourage you to explicitly put the `return` statement. We can define `main`, in any of the following two ways:

```
int main();                    // 0 ARGUMENTS
int main(int argc, char *argv[]); // 2 ARGUMENTS
```

Receiving either zero or two parameters.

✓ Value of `argc` is non-negative, representing size of `argv`.
✓ `argv[argc]` is NULL pointer.
✓ If `argc` is greater than zero, array members from `argv[0]` to `argv[argc-1]` (both including) contain pointer to strings. String pointed to by `argv[0]` represents program name. Strings pointed to by `argv[1]` through `argv[argc-1]` represent command-line parameters.

Compiler writers can provide more declarations of `main`. Some implementations also have third parameter that receive environment variables.

```
int main(int argc, char *argv[], char *envp[]);
```

A return from `main` is equivalent to calling `exit` function with value returned by `main` as its argument; reaching the `}` that terminate `main` returns a value `0`.

Question 5. 7: How can we change pointers passed to function as parameters?

Let us get the question right, we are talking about changing the pointer and not value-at pointer. In Code 5.4, `origPtr` is not updated.

```
void updatePtr(int *ptr){
  *ptr = 5;                  // CHANGE x
  ptr = (int*)malloc(sizeof(int));
  *ptr = 20;                 // DOES NOT CHANGE x
}
int main(){
  int x = 10;
  int *origPtr = &x;
  updatePtr(origPtr);
  printf("*origPtr: %d | x: %d ", *origPtr, x);
}
```

Code 5.4

Output: `*origPtr: 5 | x: 5`

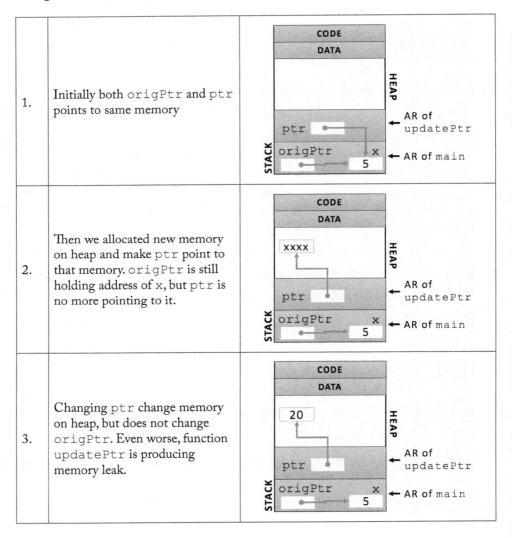

1.	Initially both `origPtr` and `ptr` points to same memory	
2.	Then we allocated new memory on heap and make `ptr` point to that memory. `origPtr` is still holding address of x, but `ptr` is no more pointing to it.	
3.	Changing `ptr` change memory on heap, but does not change `origPtr`. Even worse, function `updatePtr` is producing memory leak.	

To update `origPtr` of function `main`, we must pass address of `origPtr`, rather than `origPtr` itself.

> For calling function to be able to change a variable, we must pass address of that variable, irrespective of the type of variable.

```
void updatePtr(int **ptr){
   **ptr = 10;          // CHANGE x

   // ALLOCATE MEMORY TO origPtr
   *ptr = (int*)malloc(sizeof(int));
   **ptr = 20;          // UPDATE MEMORY OF origPtr
}
int main(){
   int x = 5;
   int *origPtr = &x;
   updatePtr(&origPtr);
   printf("*origPtr: %d | x: %d ", *origPtr, x);
}
```

Output: `*origPtr: 20 | x: 10`

This coding style is rampant while coding for data structures. Consider the structure of `Node` of linked list:

```
typedef struct node{
   int data;
   struct node* next;
}Node;
```

Let us implement a function to insert in the list maintaining it in sorted order. If `head` points to first node of list and we call the following functions:

```
Node *head = NULL;
insertSorted(head, 5);
insertSorted(head, 7);
insertSorted(head, 1);
```

Then `head` and list should be updated as follows:

We expect `head` to always point to first node of list and list is always sorted. But the computers are not (yet) intelligent enough to interpret our expectations. They interpret our code.

Without looking at implementation of function insertSorted, we can say it will not work. We are passing head and not the address-of-head to insertSorted function, insertSorted cannot change head, and head always remain NULL.

Right implementation of insertSorted must accept address of head or it should return the new head and calling function should take responsibility of updating it.

```
Node *head = NULL;
insertSorted(&head, 5);
insertSorted(&head, 7);
insertSorted(&head, 1);
```

Code 5.5 gives implementation of insertSorted function.

```
//INSERT VALUE IN SORTED LIST POINTED TO BY *hp.
void insertSorted(Node **hp, int x){
  // BOUNDARY CHECK
  if(hp == NULL){ return; }

  Node *head= *hp;

  // CREATING NEW NODE
  Node* temp = (Node*)malloc(sizeof(Node));
  temp->data = x;

  if(head == NULL || head->data > x){
    // INSERTING data AT HEAD
    temp->next = head;
    head = temp;
  }else{
    // MOVE HEAD TO POINT OF INSERTION
    while(head->next!=NULL && head->next->data<x)
      head = head->next;

    // INSERT NEW NODE AFTER HEAD
    temp->next = head->next;
    head->next = temp;
  }

  // UPDATING THE head OF main
  *hp = head;
}
```

```
// HELPER FUNCTION TO PRINT LIST.
void printList(Node *head){
  printf("LIST IS :");
  for(; head != NULL; head = head->next)
    printf("%d ",head->data);
}

int main(){
  Node* head = NULL;
  insertSorted(&head, 5);
  insertSorted(&head, 7);
  insertSorted(&head, 1);
  printList(head);
}
```

Code 5.5

Output: LIST IS :1 5 7

Question 5. 8: What is pass-by-value and pass-by-reference?

In C language, all arguments are passed by value. Reference type is available in C++, and not C. Even when we pass memory address to a function, that address is passed by value and received in a pointer variable.

```
void calledFun(int *ptr2){ … … }
void callingFun(){
  int *ptr;
  … …
  calledFun(ptr);
}
```

Both `ptr` and `ptr2` are separate variables and have their own memory. The value stored in these memories is same.

We can pass address of a local variable and change value of that variable indirectly from within `calledFun`. Some authors call this, passing of address, "pass-by-reference" because & operator is also called reference operator.

But, we should not confuse it with reference type in C++. Reference in C++, creates an alias (one more name) to the variable it refers. No extra memory is allocated to a reference.

```
int x = 5;  // int variable
int &y = x; // reference variable (C++ Code)
```

x and y are two names of same memory. No new memory is allocated to y. Compare functions to swap two integer variables written in C and C++ using pass-by-address and pass-by-reference

```
void swap(int *a,              void swap(int &a,
          int *b){                       int &b){
  int temp = *a;                 int temp = a;
  *a = *b;                       a = b;
  *b = temp;                     b = temp;
}                              }
int main(){                    int main(){
  int x = 5, y = 10;             int x = 5, y = 10;
  swap(&x, &y);                  swap(&x, &y);
}                              }
```

C Language: Pass-By-Address **C++: Pass-By-Reference**

Question 5. 9: What is a stream?

A stream is a sequence of bytes flowing into the program (input stream) or out of program (output stream).

Every stream is associated with a File when it is open. When the stream is closed, it is disassociated from the file. Loosely we can say that stream is file. In C, the term "File" can refer to a disk file, monitor, keyboard, a port, a file on tape, and so on.

fprintf function, in addition to being like printf, allows us to provide output stream to which output is sent. Following two commands does the exact same thing:

```
printf("Hello World");  // WRITE TO DEFAULT STREAM
fprintf(stdout, "Hello World"); // WRITE TO stdout
```

The printf function writes to default output stream, represented by stdout.

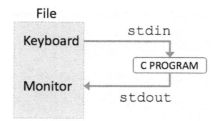

fscanf is used to receive formatted input from a given stream and fprintf is used to send formatted output to a given stream. Syntax of fscanf is similar to that of scanf. First argument of fscanf and fprintf specify stream.

```
int fscanf(FILE *fp, char *format, ...)
int fprintf(FILE *fp, char *format, ...)
```

ellipsis at the end indicate the variable number of arguments (See *Question 1.16*).

String library functions sscanf/sprintf are also similar and read/write formatted input from/to a string.

> printf = fprintf **to** stdout **stream.**
> scanf = fscanf **from** stdin **stream.**

```
int sscanf(char *str, char *format, ...)
int sprintf(char *str, char *format, ...)
```

Similarly, there are fgets and fputs corresponding to gets and puts. The routine fgetc(fp) is similar to getchar() and fputc(ch, fp) is similar to putchar(c).

fprintf can write to any stream, following code writes Hello World in file abc.txt.

```
FILE* fp;
fp = fopen("abc.txt", "w");
fprintf(fp, "Hello World");
```

fopen opens a file and associate a stream with it. Structure FILE is defined in header stdio.h. Following code opens file abc.txt created by the above code, read the contents character-by-character and print them to the console (default output stream).

```
int ch;
FILE *fp = fopen("abc.txt", "r");
while ( (ch = fgetc(fp)) != EOF )
  putchar(ch);
fclose( fp );
```

EOF is a special character that indicate End-Of-File. If file abc.txt does not exist, the code will crash because fp is NULL and we have not put any checks for that.

```
int ch ;
FILE *fp = fopen("abc.txt", "r");
if(fp != NULL){
  while ( ( ch = fgetc(fp)) != EOF )
    putchar(ch);
fclose( fp );
```

6.

BIT TWIDDLING

Question 6. 1: What is masking and how is it used?

We saw this truth table in *Question 2.1*

A	B	!A	A & B	A | B	A ^ B
0	0	1	0	0	0
0	1	1	0	1	1
1	0	0	0	1	1
1	1	0	1	1	0

Result of AND is 1 if both bits are 1 and result of OR operator is 1 if at least one of the two bits is 1. When a bit-wise operator is applied on two integers, it is applied on all the corresponding bits of those integers. Expression

```
a = 9 | 2;
```

will make value of a equal to 11.

```
        9 = ...0000001001
        2 = ...0000000010
    9 | 2 = ...0000001011 = 11.
```

Ellipsis (…) in binary representation are because we do not know exact number of bits int occupy in memory.

Bitwise operators work at bit level. A mask is a sequence of bits that allows us to perform some operation on a selected bit (instead of entire number). Mask for nth bit is

```
unsigned int mask = 1<<n;
```

all bits in mask are zero except nth bit (from right). This mask can be used to set, reset or toggle nth bit of an integer variable. Let us take a variable, x with following bit sequence

```
x = ...0000101011
```

Value of x is 43. To operate on 4th bit from right
we need the following mask

...0000101011

↑

```
unsigned int mask = 1<<4;
```

Binary representation of mask has 4th bit (starting from 0) set.

```
mask = ...0000010000
```

There are for operations that can be performed on any bit, Set (make it
1), Reset (make it 0), Toggle (if 1 make it 0, and vice-versa). Code 6.1 has
all the functions

```
// SET n'th BIT OF x
int setBit(int x, unsigned int n){
  unsigned int mask = 1<<n;
  return x|mask;  // SET THE n'th BIT
}

// RESET n'th BIT OF x
int resetBit(int x, unsigned int n){
  unsigned int mask = 1<<n;
  // ~mask HAVE n'th BIT 0, ALL OTHERS 1
  return x & (~mask);
}

// TOGGLE n'th BIT OF n
int toggleBit(int x, unsigned int n){
  unsigned int mask = 1<<n;
  return x^mask;
}
```

Code 6.1

If nth bit of x is already set, setBit function return x unchanged. Similarly,
if nth bit of x is already 0, resetBit returns x unchanged. Notice that we
are not changing value of x inside function.

To toggle the nth bit, use XOR operator. From the truth table, we know that
XOR with 1 toggle the bit and XOR with 0 leaves it unchanged.

Bitwise NOT toggle all bits in binary representation of a number. We
want to toggle only a particular bit.

Question 6. 2: What is the difference between logical-NOT and bitwise-NOT operators?

Logical NOT, ! operator considers only logical value and not the actual value of operand. For !, both 5 and 6 are same because both are true, so are 0 and (int*)0 because both are false.

```
!5 == !6 == !15
```

But for bitwise NOT operator, ~5 and ~6 are different, being one's complement of binary representations of 5 and 6 respectively. Following expression is true

```
~(~x) == x
```

Because one's complement of a binary number is equal to number itself. But, same may not be true for logical NOT operator. If x=5,

$$!(!5) = !(0) = 1 \neq x$$

!!(x) is equal to x only if x is either 0 or 1.

Moreover bitwise NOT, ~ can only be applied on integrals, whereas logical NOT, ! can take even float, double or pointer operators.

The result of logical NOT operator is either 0 or 1. For that matter, result of all logical operators is either 0 or 1 (false or true). Result of bitwise NOT can be any integral value.

You should be cautious while using bitwise operators in logical expressions because, logical NOT applied on a true value is false, but bitwise NOT applied on a true value may be true.

Question 6. 3: Write a function that returns n^{th} bit in binary representation of an integral.

To get n^{th} bit, we use the mask discussed in *Question 6.1*. Following function returns the value of nth bit in x from right

```
int getBit(int x, unsigned int n){
    unsigned int mask = 1<<n;
    return (x & mask) != 0;
}
```

If nth bit is set, value of (x & mask) is non-zero. Note that the precedence of & is less than !=. If bracket is not put, expression is evaluated as (x & (mask != 0)).

Question 6. 4: Get lowest set bit of a number.

Let us understand it with an example. If x=10, i.e. 00001010, One's complement of x is 11110101 and two's complement is 11110110. There are two ways to get 2's complement of a binary number.

1. 2's Complement = 1's Complement + 1
2. To get 2's complement keep writing bits of number from right side one by one till lowest set bit is reached. After writing the lowest set bit, toggle all other bits (on left of lowest set bit).

The only set-bit that is same in both x and -x is the lowest set bit. If we bitwise-AND original number, x with its two's complement, we get a number which has only the lowest bit of x set.

It assumes that the architecture is using two's complement notation to sore signed integers, this is a reasonably fair assumption.

```
int lowestSetBit(int x){
   return x & (-x);
}
```

Question 6. 5: Reset the lowest set bit of a number. If number is 00001010 then result should be 00001000.

In binary representations of any two consecutive numbers (x and x-1), If nth bit from right is lowest set bit in x.

1. nth bit is not set in x-1.
2. All bits to the left of nth bit are same in both x and x-1.
3. All bits to the right of nth bit are set in x-1 (and reset in x).

Lowest set bit

```
  x:  0011101000
x-1:  0011100111
```

A bitwise AND between x and x-1 reset the lowest set bit in x and keep all other bits in x unchanged.

```
int clearLowestBit(int x){
    return x & (x-1);
}
```

Question 6. 6: How do you check if a number is power of two or not? 4, 8, 1024 etc. are powers of two, 6, 40, 95 etc. are not.

A number is power of two, iff there is only one bit set in its binary representation. Question can be rephrased as, how will you check if only one bit is set in binary representation of a number?

Method-1: Take log base-2.

This is pure mathematical solution. If log2(n) is integer then n is a power of 2, else not.

Method-2: Keep dividing by 2

Keep dividing number by two (n = n/2) iteratively until n becomes 1. In any iteration, if n becomes odd (n≠1) then it is not a power of 2. If n becomes 1 (without ever becoming odd) then it is a power of 2.

```
bool powerOfTwo(int n)
{
    if(((n%2 != 0 && n != 1) || n<=0)){ return 0; }

    while(n != 1){
        n = n/2;
        if(n%2 != 0 && n != 1)
            return 0;
    }
    return 1;
}
```
                        Code 6.2

This code takes `O(lg(n))` time. Using bitwise operation, we can check in constant time as shown in Method-3.

Method-3: Use Bitwise operators

This method use the fact that, only 1 bit is set in binary representation of a number when it is power of two. If we reset the lowest set bit of number, it becomes zero (because only one bit is set).

Hence, if a number N, is power of 2 then (N & (N-1)) is zero.

The only exception to above rule is when N itself is zero. (0&-1) gives 0, but it is not power of two. This case can be handled separately

```
int powerOfTwo(int n){
   return n && (!(n & (n-1)));
}
```

This method takes constant time and constant extra memory. I have seen some companies asking the meaning of the following expression in their written test.

```
n && (!(n & (n-1)))
```

Question 6. 7: Count set bits in an integer.

Given an `unsigned int`, write code that compute number of set bits in its binary representation.

We saw in *Question 6.5* how to reset the lowest set bit in a number. If we reset set bits repeatedly, number will eventually become zero. When it becomes zero, the number of bits that we had reset gives count of bits in its binary representation:

```
int setBitsCount(int x){
   int cnt=0;
   for(; x!=0; x &= (x-1))
     cnt++;
   return cnt;
}
```

Question 6. 8: Add two numbers without using arithmetic operator.

Using bitwise operators, we can add individual bits of two numbers. While adding two bits, the SUM and CARRY bits are as follows:

```
x    y    SUM   CARRY
--   --   ---   -----
0    0    0     0
0    1    1     0
1    0    1     0
1    1    0     1
```

The SUM-bit is XOR of x and y and CARRY-bit is their bitwise-AND.

This logic (of adding two bits) can be extended for large integers. We use the fact that if corresponding bits of two integers are different then XOR (^) returns their sum and there is no carry.

```
a = 5  = 0101
b = 10 = 1010
--------------
   XOR  = 1111 = 15  (5+10)
```

If some of their bits are same, then we get carry of all common bits by taking their bitwise-AND. Following algorithm works to compute the sum

```
sum = a;
while(b != 0)
   carry = a AND b
   sum = sum XOR b
   b = carry << 1
```

Note that carry of position i gets added to position (i+1), that's why we left shift the carry. Code 6.3 has code for this algorithm
unsigned int add(unsigned int a, unsigned int b)

```
{
   while (b != 0)
   {
      int carry = a & b;
      a = a ^ b;
      b = carry << 1;
```

```
    }
    return a;
}
```

Code 6.3

Question 6. 9: Given an `unsigned int n`, find the smallest integer greater than or equal to n which is a power of 2. For example:

Input	Output
6	8
64	64

Input	Output
12	16
30	32

A power of 2 only has one bit set in its binary representation. We have to find a number greater than or equal to n with only one bit set in its binary representation.

Such a number can be found by right-shifting 1 till it becomes greater than or equal to n.

```
unsigned int nextPowerOfTwo(unsigned int n)
{
  // If n is a power of 2 then return n itself
  if (n && !(n & (n - 1)))
    return n;

  unsigned int result = 1;
  while (result < n)
    result <<= 1;
  return result;
}
```

Question 6. 10: Given two unsigned integers, how can you find greater and smaller of the two without comparing them?

This is a trick question. Trick questions are rarely asked in Coding Interviews, but it is always good to know them.

If integers are a and b, greater and smaller can be computed as follows:
```
unsigned int a, b;

// COMPUTING SMALLER
int small = b ^ ( (a^b) & -(a<b) );

// COMPUTING GREATER
int big = a ^ ( (a^b) & -(a<b) );
```

Question 6. 11: Write a function to compute xn.

Signature of function is

```
int power(int x, unsigned int n);
```

We discuss multiple methods to compute the power below.

Method-1: Brute Force - O(n) time

The brute force method for this is to use a loop as in Code 6.4

```
int power(int x, unsigned int n)
{
  int product = 1;
  for(int i=0; i<n; i++)
    product = product * x;
  return product;
}
```

Code 6.4

We can also write it recursively. Recursion is almost always less optimal than non-recursive version in terms of both time and memory, but it is such a powerful tool that you should be comfortable in writing recursive code.

```
int power(int x, unsigned int n)
{
  if (n == 0)      // TERMINATING CONDITION
    return 1;
  return x * power(x, n-1);
}
```

Code 6.5

Like non-recursive code, recursive code also takes O(n) time. But, recursive code also take O(n) memory.

Method-2: Optimal Solution - O(lg(n)) time

A Better Solution is to do *Exponentiation by Squaring* (See, https://en.wikipedia.org/wiki/Exponentiation_by_squaring). It takes advantage of the basic formula:

```
xn+m = xm * xn
```

Hence,
```
xn = xn/2 * xn/2       (If n is even)
xn = x * xn/2 * xn/2   (If n is odd)
```
Code 6.6 computes power using this logic.
```
int power(int x, unsigned int n){
  if( n == 0)
    return 1;

  int retValue = 1;
  while(n){
    if(n%2)
      retValue = retValue * x;
    x = x * x;
    n = n/2;
  }
  return retValue;
}
```

Code 6.6

The recursive version of Code 6.6 is given in Code 6.7:

```
int power(int x, unsigned int n){
  if( n == 0)
    return 1;

  int temp = power(x, n/2);

  if (n%2 == 0)
    return temp*temp;
```

```
   else
      return x*temp*temp;
}
```

Code 6.7

Note that code 6.7 is not same as Code 6.8 (though both are recursive and both does exponential multiplication).

```
int power(int x, unsigned int n){
   if (n == 0)
      return 1;

   if(n%2 == 0)
      return power(x, n/2) * power(x, n/2);
   else
      return x * power(x, n/2) * power(x, n/2);
}
```

Code 6.8

In Code 6.8 function `power` is called twice and hence it is much more time consuming. (if n=10) then `power(x,5)` will be called twice. This will also have overlapping subproblems (*For overlapping subproblems, Optimal substructure, Memoization and Dynamic programming, read our book, "Dynamic programming for Coding Interviews"*).

Question 6. 12: Computing 2^n.

This is a special case of *Question 6.11*. When we do right shift, all the bits are shifted toward right. Since each bit represent a power of two, shifting one bit right has an effect of division-by-two. If x=5 then both the following statements have same effect:

```
x = x>>1;   // 101 becomes 010 (i.e. 2)
x = x/2;    // 5/2 is 2
```

Similarly, the effect of left shift is same as multiplication-by-two (because all bits move to their higher place values). x<<1 is same as x*2.

2n can be computed in a single expression 1<<n.

```
unsigned int powerOfTwo(unsigned int n){
```

```
    return 1<<n;
}
```

This function takes constant time (much faster then single arithmetic operation). Compare it with the normal `o(n)` solution using a loop

```
int product = 1;
for(int i=0; i<n; i++)
    product = product * 2;
```

or even a `o(lg(n))` time solution discussed in *Question 6.11.*

Question 6. 13: Check for Odd-Even.

Bitwise operators are faster than arithmetic operators. If something can be done using bit-operation, then it should be preferred.

An odd number always have a set bit (1) in its Least significant bit and even number always have a zero in its least significant bit. This simple fact can be used to check if number is odd or even.

```
bool isOdd(unsigned int x){
    return (x&1 == 1);
}
```

Note that even the following function takes constant time using modulus operator (%), but absolute time taken will be little more.

```
bool isOdd(unsigned int x){
    return (x%2 == 1);
}
```

Similar approach can be used in other operations also. For example, following function converts a character from upper case to lower case:

```
char toLowerCase(char ch){
    return ch - ('a' - 'A');
}
```

To reduce an operation, we can precompute (`'a'- 'A'`) and replace it with the constant.

```
char toLowerCase(char ch){
   return ch - 32;
}
```

If this function is called very often, then even a small optimization in this function can improve overall performance of the code.

Difference between the lower case and upper case is 32, and 32 is value of bit at position 25. Bit representation of upper case and lower case alphabets are:

A:	01000001	**a:**	01100001
B:	01000010	**b:**	01100010
C:	01000011	**c:**	01100011
.	.	.	.
.	.	.	.
.	.	.	.
Z:	01011010	**z:**	01111010

The 5th bit in upper case characters is set and it is reset in lower case characters. All other bits are same for corresponding characters. Changing from upper-case to lower-case just require us to set the 5th bit. Similarly, converting from lower-case to upper-case can be done by resetting the 5th bit. Setting and resetting of a particular bit is discussed in *Question 6.1*.

Question 6. 14: Find the missing number.

Given an array of size n, having integers between 1 and n+1. There are no duplicates in the array and exactly one number from 1 to n+1 is missing.

Find missing number. For example, if n=7 and array is:

```
{8, 3, 5, 7, 4, 6, 1}
```

then the output should be 2, because 2 is missing from list of 1 to 8.

The brute force way of doing this is to search for each i from i=1 to i=n+1 one at a time and return the missing number.

```
int searchMissing(int * arr, int n){
   for(int x=1; x<=n+1; x++){
      int i=0;
      for(; i<n; i++){
```

```
      if(arr[i] == x)
        break;
    }
    if(i==n)
      return x;
  }
  return -1; // CONTROL NEVER REACH HERE
}
```

This solution takes O(n2) time in worst case. A faster solution is to use a hash table and store number of occurrences of each element in that hash. Then traverse the hash and see where the hole is.

```
int searchMissingHash(int * arr, int n){
  int hash[n]; // HASH TO STORE COUNT

  // INITIALIZE WITH ZERO
  for(int i=0; i<n; i++)
    hash[i] = 0;

  // POPULATE HASH
  for(int i=0; i<n; i++)
    hash[arr[i]-1]++;

  // CHECK HASH
  for(int i=0; i<n; i++)
    if(hash[i] == 0)
      return i+1;

  return -1; // UNREACHABLE CODE
}
```

Above solution takes O(n) time and O(n) extra memory. A better solution is to add all elements of array and subtract this sum from sum of first n+1 natural numbers. Sum of first n natural numbers can be computed in constant time using following formula from our knowledge of mathematics:

$$\sum_{k=1}^{n} k = \frac{n * (n + 1)}{2}$$

Function to find missing number is now straightforward linear time function as follows:

```
int searchMissingSum(int * arr, int n){
    int sum = 0;
    for(int i=0; i<n; i++)
        sum += arr[i];
    return ((n+1)*(n+2))/2 - sum;
}
```

Another way of solving it is using bitwise XOR operator. Following two equations are `true` for any unsigned integral X.

```
X^X = 0
X^0 = X
```

If we do XOR of all elements of array and all numbers from 1 to n+1, we get the missing number.

```
int xor = (8^3^5^7^4^6^1)^(1^2^3^4^5^7^8);
```

Value of `xor` after above operations is 2 (XOR of an element with itself is zero).

```
int searchMissingXor(unsigned int * arr, int n){
    unsigned int res = 0;
    for(int i=0; i<n; i++)
        res ^= arr[i] ^ (i+1);
    return res^(n+1);
}
```

Question 6. 15: All elements in an integer array are repeating even number of times, except for one which is repeating odd number of times. Find the number repeating odd number of times.

If the given array is

```
int arr[] = {2, 3, 2, 4, 1, 5, 3, 5, 1, 2, 4};
```

Then output should be 2, because it is repeating odd number of times.

The simplest linear solution for this problem is to perform XOR of all the numbers. The numbers repeating even number of times will cancel each other (because a^a is 0).

```
int xor = 0;
for(int i=0; i<n; i++)
  xor ^= arr[i];
```

Value of xor is the number that is repeating odd number of times.

Question 6. 16: Find the missing and repeating number.

Given an unsorted array of size n with numbers from 1 to n. One number from the set {1, 2, 3, …, n} is missing in array and only one number occurs twice. Find the repeating and missing number.

For example: If n=6, and array is

```
int arr[] = {1, 5, 3, 4, 1, 2};
```

Your code should print 6(missing) and 1(repeating). Obviously, there are multiple solutions to this problem. Let us take them one-by-one:

Method-1: Using Sorting

Sort the array and traverse it linearly to find these numbers.

```
Time taken: O(n.lg(n))
Extra Space required: Constant
```

Solution-2: Using Hashing

Use an extra array of size n and store the count of occurrences of i at ith position in array.

```
Time taken: O(n)
Extra Space Required: O(n)
```

Solution-3: Using XOR

Let us understand this solution with an example. Let the given array be

```
int a[] = {1, 5, 3, 4, 1, 2};
```

Take XOR of all elements in the array

```
xor = a[0] ^ a[1] ^ a[2] ^ a[3] ^ a[4] ^ a[5];
```

Now XOR all numbers from 1 to n with above xor

```
xor = xor ^ 1 ^ 2 ^ 3 ^ 4 ^ 5 ^ 6;
```

Final value of xor (after above operations) is XOR of missing number (6) and repeating number (1). All other elements nullify themselves.

To generalize, let us call missing number x and repeating number y. So, in effect, we got

```
xor = x ^ y;
```

All set bits in xor are either set in x or y but not both. Take any set-bit (let us take rightmost set-bit for this example, but you can take any set bit) and divide array elements in two sets A and B as follows:

✓ **Set-A:** elements of array for which that bit is set
✓ **Set-B:** elements of array for which that bit is NOT set

From our example:

```
xor = 1 ^ 6 = 111 (in binary)
```

Dividing elements on basis of their LSB

```
A = {1, 5, 3, 1}
B = {4, 2}
```

Note: We are keeping repeated number twice (different from definition of set in Mathematics).

Also divide numbers from 1 to n using same logic as above (rightmost bit value). The 2 sets now become:

```
A = {1, 5, 3, 1, 1, 3, 5}
B = {4, 2, 2, 4, 6}
```

Now, XOR of all elements of set A gives 1 (repeating element) and XOR all elements of B gives 6 (missing element). Hence, the result. Time and Space complexities of this approach are amazingly good.

```
Time taken: O(n)
Extra Space Required: Constant
```

Code 6.9 prints repeating and missing numbers in array:

```c
void getMissingAndRepeating(int *arr, int n)
{
  int xors = 0;
  int i;
  int x = 0;
  int y = 0;
  // XOR OF ALL ELEMENTS IN ARRAY
  for(i=0; i<n; i++)
    xors = xors ^ arr[i];

  // XOR OF NUMBERS FROM 1 TO n
  for(i=1; i<=n; i++)
    xors = xors ^ i;
  int setBitNum = xors & ~ (xors-1);

  // DIVIDING IN TWO SETS AND GETTING THE XORs
  for(i = 0; i < n; i++){
    if(arr[i] & setBitNum)
      x = x ^ arr[i]; // arr[i] BELONGS TO SET A
    else
      y = y ^ arr[i]; // arr[i] BELONGS TO SET B
  }

  for(i = 1; i <= n; i++){
    if(i & setBitNum)
      x = x ^ i; // arr[i] BELONGS TO SET A
    else
      y = y ^ i; // arr[i] BELONGS TO SET B
  }
  printf("Repeating: %d \nMissing: %d", x, y);
}
```

Code 6.9

Question 6. 17: Function `randomBit()` is a Random number generator that generates 0 or 1 with equal probability. Write a function using `randomBit()`, that generate 0 and 1 with 25% and 75% probability respectively.

Following function returns 1 with 75% probability and 0 with 25% probability.

```
int random(){
    return (randomBit() || randomBit());
}
```

We are calling `randomBit()` function twice, it has equal chances of returning 0 and 1. There are four possible permutations of result of these two `randomBit` functions, 00, 01, 10 and 11 (first bit represent output of first `randomBit` function, on the left of || and second bit represent output of second `randomBit` function, on the right of ||)

Only in one case out these four (when both values are zero) the result of `random` function is zero, in other three cases, it will be 1. Hence, the probability of getting a zero from `random` function is 25% and that of getting a one is 75%.

7.

LEFT OVER

Question 7. 1: Is it better to use global variable or pass parameters to function?

"Avoid global variables", is an advice that most sane people will give you. One way to implement a Binary tree, is to define the root pointer as global, another way is to define it in a function and pass it as parameter to other tree functions.

```
typedef struct node{
   int data;
   struct Node *left;
   struct Node *right;
}Node;
Node* root;

void inOrder(){
   ... ...
}
int main(){

   ... ...
   inOrder();
}
```
1. root is Global

```
typedef struct node{
   int data;
   struct Node *left;
   struct Node *right;
}Node;

void inOrder(Node * r){
   ... ...
}
int main(){
 Node* root;

   ... ...
   inOrder();
}
```
2. root is Local

If variable root is available in global scope, it can be changed by any function. When root is defined inside a function, its change can be controlled.

```
// declare global variable
int gVar=1;
... ... ...
void fun(){
   ... ... ...
```

```
if(gVar == 1){
   ... ... ...
  }
}
```

If value of gVar is not 1 and code inside if block is not executed, then it becomes very difficult to find where gVar is changed, because any function can change it. Debugging may become a nightmare, if this variable is accidentally changed in any function. Worse is when some pointer may be pointing to this global variable.

Another problem with global variables is that they are allocated memory for entire life of program. If a variable is required only for limited time, it is a memory overhead to define it global.

Moreover, if variable with a particular name is defined in global scope, then that name cannot be used anywhere else in the program (a local variable can be defined with the same name, but it may be error-prone).

Global names are good for defining global constant values, but for variables, we should prefer local scope and pass them as parameters to functions.

Even if we have to use global variable, it is a good practice to encapsulate their access in functions. Languages like C++ and Java has concept of getter/setter methods. In C we can define global variable as static (private within file) and define getter/setter functions in that file.

```
static int gVar;
int getGVar(){
   return gVar;
}
void setGVar(int v){
   gVar = v;
}
```

Using static global variable is better than using global variables.

As a thumb rule, variables should have as smaller scope as possible and if you must use global variables, document them properly.

On a lighter note,
   Question: What is the best naming prefix for a global variable?
   Answer: //

Question 7. 2: What are the common sources of error in C language?

Following are some of the common sources of error:

1. Non-terminated comment:

Single line comments came later in C, prior versions only allowed multi-line comments. But multi-line comments may result in error,

```
x=y; /* Comments not terminated
a=b; /* a=b never happens */
```

Second line is part of comment itself. a=b never happens. Luckily, most IDE's come with syntax highlighters and makes it easy to separate comment from code. Otherwise, such errors are very difficult to debug.

2. Faulty expressions:

Particularly in comparison expressions, we either miss some characters

```
if (a=b)    // ASSIGNMENT IN PLACE OF EQUAL-TO
```

or write characters in different order

```
if(a =! b) // EVALUATED AS (a = (!b))
```

or we write an expression that is logically wrong but semantically accepted by the language.

```
if(10 < a < 20)   // CONDITION ALWAYS TRUE
```

People from maths background may put such condition

```
10 < a < 20
```

to check range of a, and expect it to be true only if a is between 10 and 20. But this expression is always true. Because it is evaluated as ((10<a)<20). (10<a) is either true or false, which is either 1 or 0, both being less than 20.

Most compilers warn us against such faulty expressions, make sure not to ignore compiler warnings.

3. Order of evaluation

Order of evaluation of some operands is not defined in C language. This is discussed in detail in *Question 2.3*.

The order of evaluation of function parameters is also not defined, so even if the following code is printing right result for you, it is a bad code and its result is unspecified:

```
printf("%d, %d, %d", ++x, x++, ++x);
```

As a thumb rule never change the value of variable in a statement that is also using it in the same statement.

Operators like && and || define the order of evaluations of operands, but they may result in side effects because of short-circuit-evaluation.

4. Accidental placement of semicolon or missing braces

This can happen anywhere, but it is most common after loop, because it goes undetected there. Following loop is an infinite loop:

```
int i = 1, x=9;
while(i<=10);
{
   printf("%d * %d = %d", x, i, x*i);
   i++;
}
```

We may expect it to print mathematical table of 9, but that small little semicolon after while loop detach the body from the loop. Semicolon (NULL statement) becomes body of loop and loop becomes infinite.

Imagine you want to express love to your wife by printing "I LOVE YOU" in an infinite loop and you end up writing

```
while(true);
   printf("I LOVE YOU");
```

Your I LOVE YOU won't be printed even once.

It is also common to miss putting statements in a block. Following loop is also infinite loop because the increment of loop variant is outside the body of loop:

```
int i = 1, x=9;
while(i<=10)
  printf("%d * %d = %d", x, i, x*i);
  i++;
```

There can be many such accidents, you miss a `break` in a switch-case.

```
switch(option)
{
  case 2:
    printf("TWO");        // MISSED break
  case 3:
    pritnf("THREE");
    break;
}
```

or a Dangling-else problem discussed in *Question 2.6*.

5. De-Referencing dangling pointers or wrong pointer

Dangling pointers are discussed in detail in *Chapter-3*. There may be places where we accidentally refer a wrong pointer. Code 7.1 is to print all elements of array:

```
int arr[] = {5, 4, 3, 2, 1};
for(int i=0; i<5; i++)
  printf("%d ", *arr + i);
```

Code 7.1

But it prints 5 6 7 8 9 instead of 5, 4, 3, 2, 1 because we miss parenthesis in *(arr + i).

6. Not checking pointer parameters against NULL.

When a function receives pointer arguments, we must check those arguments to be not-null before dereferencing them. For example, if we have implemented `swap` function as follows:

```
void swap(int *a, int *b){
  int temp = *a;
  *a = *b;
```

```
   *b = temp;
}
```

This `swap` function will crash if it is called like

```
swap(NULL, NULL);
```

The compiler will pass it because `NULL` is a valid value for pointer parameters.

No matter what the input should be, our function should never crash. A better way to implement this function is as follows:

```
void swap(int *a, int *b){
  if(a==NULL || b==NULL) { return; }
  int temp = *a;
  *a = *b;
  *b = temp;
}
```

In fact, this thing is valid for all parameters, you should check them for logically valid values. For example, if variable x has to be always positive, then we should either receive it in an `unsigned int` or we must check it.

```
void fun(int x){
  if(x<=0){
    printf("Invalid value");
    return;
  }
  … … …
}
```

The most common usage is to check variable to be non-zero before using it as denominator.

```
if(b != 0)
  x = a/b;
```

7. Integer division

If both operands are `int`, result is also `int`. In the following code the value of x is `2.0` (and not `2.5`) because expression on right side is integer expression which results in `2`, and then this `2` is converted to `double`.

```
int a = 5, b = 2;
double x = a/b;
```

In such a situation, we must force the compiler to perform the division of real number (instead of integer-division).

```
double x = (double)a/b;
```

In most cases, integer division is used as a feature. In code 7.2 this feature of integer division is used along with modulus operator to reverse digits of a number.

```
unsigned int reverseDigits(unsigned int x){
  int rev = 0;
  while(x >0){
    rev = rev*10 + x%10; // ADD LSD TO rev
    x = x/10;           // int DIVISION BY 10
  }
  return rev;
}

int main(){
  printf("%d ", reverseDigits(1234));
}
```

Code 7.2

Function reverseDigits works fine because of integer division.

8. Using strict equality with floating points

We saw in *Question 2.1*, how the following for loop becomes infinite

```
for(f = 0.1; f != 1.0; f = f + 0.1)
  printf("Love");
```

Similarly, following code fall into the else clause and print "Bye", rather than a "Hello".

```
float x = 1.2;
if(x == 1.2)
  printf("Hello");
else
  printf("Bye");
```

This is because, we are comparing float variable x with double value 1.2 (See *Question 1.9*).

9. Returning garbage from a function.

Following function doubles the value when it is less than 100

```
int doubleValue(int x){
   if(x<100)
      return x*x;
}
```

when x is less than 100, it works fine, but when x is greater than or equal to 100, the value returned is garbage. In the latest compilers, it will be flagged as error.

10. High nested indentation.

This is not an error, but if your code has very high nesting, indented code may become difficult to read because of limited width of screen.

```
for(){
    if(){
        while(){
            if(){
                for(){
                    ... ... // TOO MUCH NESTING
                }
            }
        }
    }
}
```

If your logic demands this, then it is better to take some of the nesting to a function:

```
void func(){
    while(){
        if(){
```

```
            for(){
                ... ...
            }
        }
    }
}
... ...
for(){
    if(){
        func();
    }
}
```

11. Choose meaningful variable names

This is also not an error. But making sensible choice of words for variable names makes a good impression in the interview.

12. Do not ignore compiler warnings

It is discussed in *Question 2.11*. Just want to emphasize it again.

Question 7. 3: How to print "Hello World" without using any semicolon?

This is a tricky question. Personally, I never ask such question in any interview. And my view is shared by many others. But, while learning C language, it is good to know as many tricks as possible.

Code 7.3 prints "Hello World" and does not have any semi-colon.

```
int main()
{
   if(!printf("Hello World")
   { }
}
```

Code 7.3

Function printf returns number of characters printed, 11 in this case, which is true. An empty block is a NULL statement.

Another such tricky question can be, Replace COND in Code 7.4, so that output is "`Hello World`".

```
if(COND)
  printf("Hello");
else
  printf("World");
```

Code 7.4

We know that a well-defined code never go in both `if` and `else` block of a condition at the same time. The only way to print `Hello World` is to print `Hello` in the COND itself.

```
if(!printf("Hello"))
  printf("Hello");
else
  printf("World");
```

`Hello` is printed in condition, and `World` gets printed in `else` part.

Such tricky questions are good for lateral thinking and many of us like to know these tricks. Let's take one more question:

Change exactly one character in Code 7.5, so that * is printed exactly 10 times

```
int main(){
  int n = 10;
  for(int i = 0; i < n; i--)
    printf("*");
}
```

Code 7.5

There are multiple ways (read, tricks) to do it, some of them are:

✓ Decrement n
```
for(int i = 0; i < n; n--)
  printf("*");
```

✓ Check with negative i
```
for(int i = 0; -i < n; i--)
  printf("*");
```

✓ Check the sum of n and i
```
for(int i = 0; i + n; i--)
  printf("*");
```

Question 7. 4: Which of the two loops will run faster?

```
for(i=0; i<n; i++)              for(i=n; i>0; i--)
  printf("*");                     printf("*");
```

Well, an interviewer in the year 2018 should not be asking this question anymore. This is a question of 20th century. But you know how interviewers are, sometimes they forget to upgrade themselves.

Long ago, when I was young, there was a common machine instruction used by assembly programmers called, "**Decrement and skip if zero**". It was used to implement loops. And because of this instruction, comparison with zero (to end loop) was little faster than comparison with non-zero.

There are still some processors (and some professors) on which it is cheaper to compare with zero than with anything else.

Coming from that background, down-to loop (on right side) is slightly better than the other one, but there is hardly any measurable difference.

Personally, I prefer the usual loop

```
for(i=0; i<n; i++)
  printf("*");
```

because, it is not just easier (implement down-to-zero loop from 50 to 80) but also more readable.

Question 7. 5: How is `const` qualifier used in C language?

As the name suggests, const qualifier can be used with identifiers to indicate that their values cannot be changed.

```
const int x = 10;

x = 5; // ERROR. Cannot change const identifiers
```

Identifiers defined as const cannot be changed directly but, C being a funny language, allows to change constants indirectly thru pointers.

```
const int x = 10;
x = 5;          // ERROR.
```

```
int *ptr = &x;
*ptr = 20;  // OK. VALUE OF x CHANGED TO 20.
```

It can be understood in a way that qualifier `const` is not attached with memory. It just qualifies the identifier name. `x` as an identifier is non-modifiable, but same qualifier is not applied to memory.

When a pointer is defined as `const` then depending on where the qualifier is placed, either pointer or value-pointed-to-by-it is constant.

```
int x = 10; int y = 20;

//can't change *ptr but can change ptr itself
const int *ptr = &x;
ptr = &y; // OK
*ptr = 5; // ERROR

//Can't change ptr1 itself, but can change *ptr1
int * const ptr1 = &x;
ptr1 = &x; // ERROR
*ptr1 = 5; // OK
```

The way to read such definitions is to start with the identifier and move leftward.

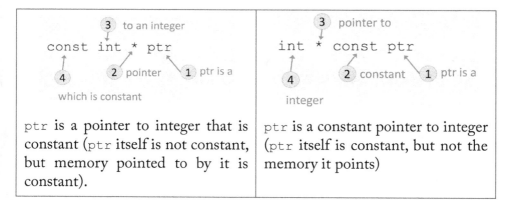

`ptr` is a pointer to integer that is constant (`ptr` itself is not constant, but memory pointed to by it is constant).	`ptr` is a constant pointer to integer (`ptr` itself is constant, but not the memory it points)

Definition `int const *ptr;` is also same as `const int *ptr;`. Try reading both of them, they will sound similar. Now read following definition.

```
const int *const ptr;
```

`ptr` is a constant pointer to integer that is also constant. It means, both `ptr` and value-at-`ptr` are constant and cannot be modified.

> In C++ you cannot modify a const object either directly or indirectly. Because address of const variable can only be assigned to const pointers.

Question 7. 6: What is the output of following program?

```
int main()
{
  goto INSIDE_LOOP;
  {
    int x = 15;        // UNREACHABLE CODE
INSIDE_LOOP:
    printf("%d", x);
  }
  return 0;
}
```

x is a local variable, it is allocated memory in the activation record of function. Because we are directly jumping to the printf statement, initialization of x is skipped and the value of x remains garbage. Hence, output is garbage.

Question 7. 7: If ptr is a pointer to array, then what is the difference between ++*ptr and *ptr++?

```
int main()
{
  int arr[] = {1, 2};
  int *ptr = arr;

  ++*ptr;
  printf("arr[0]: %d arr[1]: %d *ptr: %d\n",
         arr[0], arr[1], *ptr);

  arr[0] = 1; arr[1] = 2;   // RESETING
  ptr = arr;
  *ptr++;
  printf("arr[0]: %d arr[1]: %d *ptr: %d\n",
```

```
            arr[0], arr[1], *ptr);

    arr[0] = 1; arr[1] = 2;  // RESETING
    ptr = arr;
    *++ptr;
    printf("arr[0]: %d arr[1]: %d *ptr: %d\n",
            arr[0], arr[1], *ptr);
}
```

Code 7.6

The output of Code 7.6 is

```
arr[0]: 2 arr[1]: 2 *ptr: 2
arr[0]: 1 arr[1]: 2 *ptr: 2
arr[0]: 1 arr[1]: 2 *ptr: 2
```

From *Question 2.1*, we know that:

✓ Precedence of pre-increment and value-at(*) is same and associativity of both is right to left.
✓ Precedence of post-increment is higher than both value-at(*) and pre-increment and associativity of post-increment is left to right.

Expression ++*p has two operators of same precedence and right to left associativity. It is evaluated as ++(*p). Same is true about *++p, and it is evaluated as * (++p).

Expression *p++ has two operators, where ++ has higher precedence than value-at. It is evaluated as * (p++).

Question 7. 8: How will you sort an array of Students on marks field? Structure of `Student` is defined as follows:

```
struct Student
{
    char name[25];
    int rollNo;
    double marks;
};
```

When we want to sort an array using quick sort, the sorting logic of quick sort remains same irrespective of data types of elements in array. But, comparator logic (the way individual elements of array are compared) may be different for different data types.

For example, if array, `arr` has simple integers then elements can be directly compared using comparison operators

```
arr[i] > arr[j]
```

But if `arr` is an array of strings, they need to be compared like strings

```
strcmp(arr[i], arr[j])
```

Similarly, if `arr` is an array of `Student`, and we want to sort on `Student.marks` field then comparator logic is

```
arr[i].marks > arr[j].marks
```

and if `arr` is an array of `Student`, and we want to sort on `Student.rollNo` field then comparator logic is as follows:

```
arr[i].rollNo > arr[j].rollNo
```

But, irrespective of how we compare individual elements of array, sorting logic remains same.

C language library comes with in-build function to sort an array. But that function does not know how to compare elements, we have to supply our own comparator logic and library will use that comparison logic to sort the array. If `arr` is an array of `Student` type

```
struct Student arr[5] = { {"Ram",    4, 80.5},
                          {"Mohan", 1, 92.5},
                          {"Shyam", 3, 79.4},
                          {"Radha", 5, 81.5},
                          {"Sita",  2, 92.6}};
```

Then, we may sort it on any of the three fields, if we want to sort it on `rollNo`, we compare individual roll numbers and if we want to sort on marks, then we compare students on marks field. Code 7.7 has the two comparators to sort on `marks` and `rollNo`.

```
// COMPARATOR FOR marks
int comparatorMarks(const void *a, const void *b)
{
    struct Student *ptr1 = (struct Student*)a;
```

```c
  struct Student *ptr2 = (struct Student*)b;

  return ptr1->marks > ptr2->marks;
}

// COMPARATOR FOR rollNo
int comparatorRollNo(const void *a, const void *b)
{
  struct Student *ptr1 = (struct Student*)a;
  struct Student *ptr2 = (struct Student*)b;

  return ptr1->rollNo > ptr2->rollNo;
}

// HELPER FUNCTION TO PRINT THE ARRAY
void printArray(struct Student *ptr, int n)
{
  for(int i=0; i<n; i++)
    printf("%d %-7s %lf\n", ptr[i].rollNo,
           ptr[i].name, ptr[i].marks);
}

int main(){
  struct Student arr[5] = { {"Ram",    4, 80.5},
                            {"Mohan", 1, 92.5},
                            {"Shyam", 3, 79.4},
                            {"Radha", 5, 81.5},
                            {"Sita",  2, 92.6}};

  printf("BEFORE SORTING:\n");printArray(arr, 5);

  // SORT ON MARKS
  qsort((void*)arr, 5, sizeof(arr[0]),
        comparatorMarks);

  printf("AFTER SORTING ON MARKS: \n");
  printArray(arr, 5);

  // SORT ON ROLL NUMBER
  qsort((void*)arr, 5, sizeof(arr[0]),
        comparatorRollNo);

  printf("AFTER SORTING ON ROLLNO: \n");
  printArray(arr, 5);
}
```

Code 7.7

Output of Code 7.7 is as follows:

```
BEFORE SORTING:
4 Ram      80.500000
1 Mohan    92.500000
3 Shyam    79.400000
5 Radha    81.500000
2 Sita     92.600000
AFTER SORTING ON MARKS:
3 Shyam    79.400000
4 Ram      80.500000
5 Radha    81.500000
1 Mohan    92.500000
2 Sita     92.600000
AFTER SORTING ON ROLLNO:
1 Mohan    92.500000
2 Sita     92.600000
3 Shyam    79.400000
4 Ram      80.500000
5 Radha    81.500000
```

If we want to arrange an array such that all even numbers come before all odd numbers, then we can define comparator in a way that even number is less than odd number and call qsort function (A better approach is to use counting sort).

Question 7. 9: What are assertions in C language?

An assertion is a logically impossible situation, such that, if that situation is true, we want the program to abort.

Assertions in C are implemented with a simple assert macro. Signature of this macro is as follows:

```
void assert( int exp );
```

If exp evaluates to 0 (false), the expression, filename, and line number are sent to standard error stream stderr, and abort() function is called that terminates the program. If exp evaluates to non-zero (true), nothing happens.

For example, if we are allocating memory in the heap

```
int *ptr = malloc(sizeof(int) * 10);
assert(ptr != NULL);
```

when `ptr` is `NULL`, program terminates. Consider the following program:

```
void func()
{
  x = 9;
  assert(x!=9);
  ... ...
}
```

The assert is an impossible situation and if x is somehow changed, the code will not move forward.

There is a difference between assertion and normal error. If a function encounter normal error, it returns with appropriate value.

```
int linearSearch(int *arr, int n, int data)
{
  if(arr == NULL)
    return -1;       // NORMAL ERROR SITUATION
  for(int i=0; i<n; i++)
    if(arr[i] == data)
      return i;
  return -1;
}
```

If `arr` is `NULL`, then it's a normal error that `linearSearch` should be able to handle gracefully.

Assertions can be disabled in production by compiling code with appropriate options. But logical errors should not be disabled.

Question 7. 10: What is the purpose of `fork()`?

`fork` is an operation in Unix (and Unix-like systems) where a process creates a copy of itself.

The new process created is called child process and the one that creates it is called parent process. Parent process continue to execute and Child process starts executing from the next statement following the `fork()` command.

It creates a separate address space for child process and all segments (data, code, stack, heap, ...) are copied to child process address space. After this point, execution of the two process is independent, and both executes concurrently.

```c
int main()
{
  printf("Before Fork \n");
  fork();
  printf("After Fork \n");
}
```

Code 7.8

Initially, only one program is executing, and it prints "Before Fork". Then fork command asks the operating system to create a new process. Once the new process is created, both of them continue their independent execution concurrently from next statement after fork and prints "After Fork". Output of Code 7.8 is

```
Before Fork
After Fork
After Fork
```

Parent Process	Child Process
`int main()`	`int main()`
`{`	`{`
`  printf("Before Fork \n");`	`  printf("Before Fork \n");`
`  fork();`	`  fork();`
`  printf("After Fork \n");`	`  printf("After Fork \n");`
`}`	`}`

```
Output
Before Fork
After Fork
After Fork
```

Note that there is no fixed order in which "After Fork" of parent and child are printed because both are independent processes. Consider the following program:

```c
int main()
```

```
{
  printf("A ");
  fork();
  printf("B ");
  fork();
  printf("C ");
}
```

The first fork command creates two processes, both of them will print "B " and both of them will fork one child process each on second fork command, resulting in four independent processes, each printing "C ".

- ✓ **P1** prints A B C
- ✓ **P2** prints B C
- ✓ **P3** and **P4** prints C

The output of processes is intermixed in an un-deterministic way depending on process context switch of operating system.

If a process has the following loop:

```
for(i=0; i<n; i++)
  fork();
```

Then total number of child processes created are 2n-1.

How do we know whether we are in parent or child process?

The return value of fork command is important.

```
int x = fork();
```

- ✓ **If x is 0,** It means that we are in child process.
- ✓ **If x is positive**, it means we are in parent process and x is the process-id of the newly created child process.

✓ **If x is negative**, it means that fork() has failed and was not able to create any child process.

In Code 7.9, parent process only prints "INSIDE PARENT", and child process only prints "INSIDE CHILD".

```
int main()
{
  if(fork()!=0)
    printf("INSIDE PARENT\n");
  else
    printf("INSIDE CHILD\n");
}
```

Code 7.9

The printf statements can be replaced by function calls to make parent and child perform separate functions.

What will be the output of the following code? Let's leave it as an exercise for you guys !

```
int main()
{
  fork();
  fork() && fork() || fork();
  fork();

  printf("Bye from Ritambhara Technologies\n");
}
```